Roger Williams's Little Book of Virtues

Roger Williams's Little Book of Virtues

— Becky Garrison —

RESOURCE *Publications* • Eugene, Oregon

ROGER WILLIAMS'S LITTLE BOOK OF VIRTUES

Copyright © 2020 Becky Garrison. All rights reserved. Except for brief quotations in critical publications or reviews, no part of this book may be reproduced in any manner without prior written permission from the publisher. Write: Permissions, Wipf and Stock Publishers, 199 W. 8th Ave., Suite 3, Eugene, OR 97401.

Resource Publications
An Imprint of Wipf and Stock Publishers
199 W. 8th Ave., Suite 3
Eugene, OR 97401

www.wipfandstock.com

PAPERBACK ISBN: 978-1-5326-9654-1
HARDCOVER ISBN: 978-1-5326-9655-8
EBOOK ISBN: 978-1-5326-9656-5

All photographs by Becky Garrison.

NakedPastor.com cartoons used with permission of David Hayward/Naked Pastor.

Manufactured in the U.S.A.   01/09/20

Contents

List of Illustrations | vi
Acknowledgements | vii

1. Reclaiming Roger | 1
2. Piecing Together the Past | 19
3. Prudence | 33
4. Justice | 47
5. Courage | 58
6. Temperance | 66
7. Roger and Me: My Journey from Christian to Spiritual Seeker | 70

Bibliography | 87

Illustrations

Oldest continuous 4th of July parade, Bristol, RI | 2

Are Trump and the Church in Bed Together? | 9

Tell the Difference | 15

Roger's final resting place in Providence, RI | 20

Pulpit Rock: On this rock Roger Williams preached to the Indian inhabitants of Prudence Island | 23

Prudence Island, RI at Sunset | 38

Paper mâché statue of Roger (1960) | 46

Are Smart Women Evil? | 54

Not Going in There with All Those Homosexuals! | 57

Warning... God will judge you | 61

Bullet Cross | 69

What to Wear | 76

Creation meets Evolution | 85

Acknowledgements

Thanks to my ancestor Roger Williams for starting this battle and to Gary Austin and Robert Darden for giving me the voice so I could present his work to a contemporary audience. And a special thank you to Edward Jacobowitz for his keen editorial eye.

1
Reclaiming Roger

[The merger of church and state remains] opposite to the souls of all men who by persecutions are ravished into a dissembled worship which their hearts embrace not.

—Roger Williams[1]

Williams is an inconvenient figure for today's religious right, which asserts that the only purpose of the "wall of separation" was to protect religion from government—not government from religion. That was true in early colonial America, but the other side of the equation was well understood by the time the Constitution—which never mentions God and explicitly bars all religious tests for public office—was written. Destructive religious wars in 17th-century Europe, among other factors, had led many Americans to the realization that governments could indeed be threatened by a close identification with religion.

—Susan Jacoby[2]

Religion easily has the greatest bullshit story ever told.

—George Carlin[3]

---

1. Estep, *Revolution Within the Revolution*, 76.
2. Jacoby, "White House Tearing Down."
3. Carlin, "Religion."

Oldest continuous 4th of July parade, Bristol, RI

IN THE 2016 UNITED States presidential election, 81 percent of white evangelicals voted for a TV reality star even though he seems to be a malignant narcissist and a sociopath.[4] These are not personality traits normally associated with the teachings of their supposed leader in heaven, Jesus of Nazareth. But I suppose these Christians have a different criteria for their actual leader here on earth. As of January 2019, 69 percent of white evangelical Protestants continue to approve of the way Trump is handling his job as president.[5] Once he exits the stage, I predict white evangelicals will continue to seek out those political candidates who will support the godawful agenda advanced by his administration.

Why is the current occupant in the White House supported by a triumvirate of right wing Christianity—American

4. See Martinez and Smith, "How the Faithful Voted" and Lee, *The Dangerous Case of Donald Trump*.

5. See Schwadel and Smith, "Evangelical Support for Trump Remains High."

evangelicalism, the prosperity gospel, and white nationalist pride?[6] What in God's name is going on?

Prior to the elevation of Trump by the majority of white evangelicals, I grew tired of satirizing this God-game, and moved on to covering other topics such as the craft culture and secular spiritualities I discovered upon moving to the Pacific Northwest. But the 2016 election stirred within me the bones of my ancestor Roger Williams. Just as he spoke out against injustices fueled by politicized religiosity, I realize I am called to do likewise.

> At a crisis when the public mind, in this and other countries, is so strongly excited on questions of civil and religious liberty, the great principle advocated by Williams—that civil rulers have no authority to prescribe, enjoin, or regulate religious beliefs—demands the most serious consideration of every church and of every government.
>
> —ROMEO ELTON, "Life of Roger Williams" (1862)[7]

To paraphrase folk icon Bob Dylan—are the times a-changin'?[8] Maybe not so much. *Plus ça change, plus c'est la même chose.* When I take the spiritual temperature of America, I feel the echoes of Roger in my bones.[9] Elton's reflections, penned over 150 years ago in reference to this seventeenth-century pioneer of religious freedom, could easily apply to contemporary debates over the role of religion in the public square.

---

6. Garrison, "Surveying the Demise."
7. Elton, *Life of Roger Williams*, iv.
8. See Dylan, "The Times They are a-Changin.'"
9. Portions of Roger's history are excerpted from Garrison, *Jesus Died for This?*, 151–158. Given the familial nature of our relationship, I refer to Roger Williams throughout this book as "Roger" unless I am quoting someone directly who uses his last name. Calling a relative by his last name seems too formal, saying my ancestor sounds too pretentious, and going with "12th great-grandfather Williams" is simply too long winded. According to family lore, I am related to Roger via his sons Joseph and Daniel. This incestuous relationship would help explain some of my extended family's dysfunction. However, my connection to Joseph appears to break down after the 4th generation, though my lineage via Daniel remains solid.

The philosopher George Santayana wrote, "Those who cannot remember the past are condemned to repeat it."[10] So before we look at our present Trumpster-dump, where a fear-based evangelical faith once again dominates the US of A from sea to shining sea, we should do a quick run through of "Americana" Christianity to understand what we can learn from our past.[11]

As Roger's direct descendant, I would like to explore what we can learn from my ancestor's life and legacy that can help us navigate through this current sociopolitical crisis. How did Roger manage to endure the trials of his life, and leave a legacy of liberty that echoes now throughout the world?

This isn't a *Farmers' Almanac*-y guidebook that serves up quotes from the past to help guide us through our contemporary problems.[12] I want to explore how Roger lived a virtuous life with an eye towards what we can glean from his actions to help us get out of this twenty-first century religious morass.

For those who think this rise of the religious right represents a new trend in Americana Christianity, history shows otherwise. The mantra of Trump's white evangelical supporters, that America should shine forth as an exemplar of the Christian faith, is at least as old as the original thirteen colonies, as when the first Governor of the Massachusetts Bay Colony, John Winthrop, wrote the famous phrase, "a city upon a hill." Far too many of them, however, believe that having faith means that God is on their side—and that therefore, everything they do is right.

In *Smithsonian* magazine, Kenneth C. Davis debunks the commonly held belief that the Pilgrims and Puritans came to America in search of authentic religious freedom where everyone could be free to worship as they please. "From the earliest arrival of Europeans on America's shores, religion has often been a cudgel, used to discriminate, suppress and even kill the foreign,

---

10. Wokeck & Coleman, eds., *Works of George Santayana*, 172.
11. See Fea, "Evangelical Fear Elected Trump."
12. *Farmers' Almanac*.

the 'heretic' and the 'unbeliever'—including the 'heathen' natives already here." [13]

Davis delineates the infighting amongst Christian factions within the individual colonies. "Moreover, while it is true that the vast majority of early-generation Americans were Christian, the pitched battles between various Protestant sects and, more explosively, between Protestants and Catholics, present an unavoidable contradiction to the widely held notion that America is a 'Christian nation.'"[14] The notion of a *unified* "Christian nation" promoted by the religious right remains a fantasy. And all of the above is a betrayal of Christianity's peaceful ideals.

The language of religion used to justify secular power is of course not a new dynamic. What was arguably new was that a colony might aspire to become the embodiment of the New Israel, in the language of the times—an attempt to live up to the highest ideals of Christianity as the colonists understood them. And they each understood them differently.

This is perhaps most obvious in the Puritans under Winthrop. "His appropriation of the language of God's chosen people, his repurposing of the scriptural text for the New Englanders' own circumstances, his reading of God's providential hand in every detail of their venture, his confidence that he could pierce the analogies between modern and biblical time: these were all audacious acts. Roger Williams quailed at the hubris."[15] In his opposition to this kind of language, Roger originated the principle of separation of church and state.[16] That principle is now part of the fabric of the modern United States, as well as many countries around the world. Even now, however, the kind of thinking Winthrop used remains prevalent among those who wish to impart their particular brand of religion onto the rest of the world.

Fast forward a few hundred years. In 1953, The Family (aka The Fellowship Foundation) began hosting the National Prayer

13. Davis, "America's True History."
14. Davis, "America's True History."
15. Rodgers, *City on a Hill*, 57.
16. See Barry, "God, Government."

Breakfast, an annual gathering of US politicians, pastors, and industry leaders. During the Eisenhower era, Americana Christianity became embedded in US civil religion. "In God We Trust" was added to the US paper currency, "Under God" became part of the Pledge of Allegiance, and evangelist Billy Graham led Christian crusades against the evils of godless Communism.[17]

This time also saw the advent of the John Birch Society and other right-wing groups that linked religion with racism in a way more acceptable to the conformist fifties than the KKK had become. Bigotry and religion, a mix again not new to America. This nation has made much progress since then in many ways. However, churches today remain nearly as segregated as water fountains and lunch counters were under Jim Crow.[18]

In recent years, I've witnessed a resurgence of a Christianized form of bigotry and hatred that I hoped went away with the fall of Joseph McCarthy.[19] When I started writing for the religious satire magazine *The Wittenburg Door* in 1994, the same year the Religious Right took over Congress, I thought we were chronicling the beginning of their end. Despite the ongoing presence of a politicized form of faith, if you had told me around 2008, when *The Wittenburg Door* closed for good, that the sociopolitical climate of the United States could get any dumber than Dubya, I would have responded, "That's a political impossibility." I would have been certain that even though we were living in such uncertain times, Americans would never be so naïve as to allow ourselves to be driven by a fear-based theology with no grounding whatsoever in Jesus of Nazareth's teachings. After a few religious right zealots blamed the Newton school shooting on the gays, I penned a piece for *Religion Dispatches* proclaiming the Religious Right dead.[20]

---

17. Part of this text is from Garrison, "Christ and Capitalism." For a brief history of The Family along with a set of links for more in-depth research see Garrison, "The Family: More Gilead than Godly."

18. Lipka, "U.S. Congregations are Still Racially Segregated."

19. For a concise exploration of McCarthyism, see Miller Center, "McCarthyism and the Red Scare."

20. See Garrison, "Obituary for Right-wing Evangelicalism?"

But I was wrong.

Since the formation of the Religious Right in the 1970s, white evangelical voters have gone from embracing the Ronald to electing the Donald.[21] During the eighties the Religious Right and Donald J. Trump rose to power, Cosby and Roseanne headlined beloved sitcoms, and Gordon Gekko in Oliver Stone's *Wall Street* assured us that greed is good. Currently, Cosby is revealed as a predator, Roseanne as a racist beloved by the alt. right, and . . . greed seems to still be good. At least some things haven't changed.[22]

Trump could easily be a character lifted from a Jonathan Swift story. Though, I suspect Swift's head would swim trying to keep track of Trump's history of unethical behavior: multiple extramarital affairs, discriminating against people of color, hanging with local mobsters, and abusing—in apparent order of increasing closeness to him—his fellow citizens, his tenants, his employees, his multiple wives, and his business associates.[23] Lord only knows how even a wordsmith as adroit as Swift could satirize the ridiculousness inherent in Trump's cabinet, Supreme Court appointments, and executive orders, as well as his faith advisory board of B and C level evangelical and prosperity gospel leaders.[24]

Even before Trump gifted comedians with antics too bizarre to satirize, we were already careening towards Christian crazytown. Who in their right mind could have predicted that a politician whose name Dan Savage turned into an Internet meme would ever be taken seriously as a presidential candidate?[25] Why

---

21. See Garrison, "From Ronald to the Donald" for an analysis of the deevolution of the Republican Party from Ronald Reagan to Donald Trump.

22. For a history of the rise of the religious right see Balmer, *Thy Kingdom Come* and Fitzgerald, *The Evangelicals*. The phrase "Greed is good" is a paraphrase of a line from the movie *Wall Street*. For details about Barr and Cosby, see Baysinger, "Flashback: Bill Cosby and Roseanne."

23. For in-depth histories of Trump's antics check out these books: Barnett, *The Greatest Show;* Kranish and Fisher, *Trump Revealed*; Johnston, *The Making of Donald Trump*; and Singer, *Trump and Me*.

24. See Zuckerman, "The Trump Administration's Alternative Christianity."

25. No, I am not about to explain this. For those who don't get the reference, Google "Santorum." Caution: NSFW.

in the name of the Abrahamic God would any sane "Christian" leader demonize women for choosing to practice responsible family planning?[26] The list could go on and on and on—but I would like to keep my lunch.

The 2008 election of Barack Obama, coupled with the rise of the "nones," Americans who profess no faith, gave rise to the notion that the most virulently racist brands of Christianity might have reached their end. However, the ongoing "birther" attacks on Obama, coupled with the white pushback against #BlackLivesMatter, illuminates how the United States is by no means color blind.[27]

Under Trump, the twenty-first century's evangelicals have been rewriting their own code of ethics to where they began to once again tout views like #WhiteLivesMatter openly. Clearly this stinky spiritual stew had been brewing for some time just waiting for someone like Trump to come along and convince enough white Christians to join him in a godawful church supper.[28]

---

26. See Catholic Answers, "Tract: Birth Control," McLain, "How the Catholic Church," and Bronner, "Religious Groups and Employers."

27. Those wishing to delve into this topic further should check out Kendi, *How to Be an Antiracist*.

28. For a history of racism in the US see Kendi, *Stamped from the Beginning*. This piece notes the US evangelical Christian response to #blacklivesmatter: Inazu, "Do Black Lives Matter." Articles that can help explain why so many so-called "Christians" voted for Donald Trump: Renault, "Myths Debunked" and Wolpe, "Who Donald Trump Would Be." For background about #WhiteLivesMatter see Southern Poverty Law Center, "White Lives Matter."

29

Concurrent with this return of a virulently racist form of fundamentalism, I see signs of hope, especially among the rise of Americans who classify their religious affiliation as "none."[30] The number of those leaving the Christian faith, and evangelicalism in particular, continues to grow.[31] Without guilt ridden dogmas, they are free to choose a path that speaks to them. Some find occasional comfort in a church, synagogue, temple, or mosque that truly welcomes all and aims to be a place of healing and not a means to harm others. Such an open stance can come at quite a great risk given the rise of shootings at religious institutions in the

---

29. Hayward, "Trump and Church in Bed."
30. See Garrison, "Rise of the Party of Nones."
31. See Burleigh, "Tump and White Evangelicals."

industrialized nations.³² Others will choose to worship, reflect, or meditate in other equally valid ways outside of traditional religious structures.³³ Also, for the first time in U.S. history, one sees atheists starting to come out of the closet in droves.

Christianity is still the dominant religion in the United States. However, signs indicate the number of those who check off "Christian" in the US Census forms will continue to fall.³⁴ But before we crack out the fine wine and raise a toast to the final demise of US right wing evangelicalism, their support that ushered Trump into the White House will enable white evangelicals to keep haunting the halls of Congress and spooking the courts for the foreseeable future.³⁵

Echoing My Ancestor Roger

In discovering the works of my ancestor, I think I may have found a way out of this missional madness. As Steve Waldman observes in *Sacred Liberty*, "[Roger's] disagreements went further, reminding us that in any period, some remarkable men and women are able to pull themselves out of context and think in shockingly modern ways."³⁶

Obviously, one cannot directly apply Roger's pre-enlightenment Puritan theology to the twenty-first century globalized pluralistic world. For starters, contemporary hot button issues like women's rights, the legacy of slavery, LGBTQ+ issues, and Islamaphobia that dominate contemporary US religio-political discourse

32. See Follman et al. "US Mass Shootings, 1982–2019."

33. On the Progressive Spirit podcast with John Shuck, I reflected on the growing rise of secular spiritual communities I've encountered in recent years with a particular focus on the Pacific Northwest. See Shuck, "Becky Garrison, Secular Church."

34. See Garrison, "Surveying the Demise," which points to the sharp rise of people who are unaffiliated with a particular religion. These numbers point more towards a rise in secularism in general rather than either atheism or agnosticism alone.

35. See Balmer, "Under Trump" and Newell, "Trump Answers Prayers."

36. Waldman, *Sacred Liberty*, 18.

were not viewed the same way in the seventeenth century. Roger and his contemporaries considered women to be their husband's property, had few qualms about owning slaves, and appear to have never discussed consensual non-heterosexuality.[37] The very words did not exist: for example, "Islam" and "Muslim" entered the English language in the seventeenth century.[38]

However, I believe Roger's bedrock determination that personal beliefs about religion were sacred and not subject to governmental control would not only survive. But were he somehow be resurrected today, he would support issues of personal integrity such as sexual orientation, gender identity, and reproductive rights.

Mind you, this doesn't mean Roger's moral code would have him going to Pride parades. This freethinker was also a diehard Calvinist with a very rigid moral code about how he chose to conduct his life. In *Godly Republicanism*, Michael P. Winship describes Roger's personal faith. "Unlike many Puritans after his conversion, he never wrestled with doubts about his salvation. But he struggled all his life to purge sin from himself and from his worship of God."[39] However, these struggles represented his personal demons that he battled in the privacy of his own soul. Roger never felt anyone else should be compelled by law to follow his particular faith journey.

This doesn't mean Roger was so live-and-let-live that he would never presume to dispute ideals with anyone. A stout sectarian, Roger never backed away from the chance to debate

---

37. These attitudes still inform the notion of "biblical marriage" being bandied about by some Christians. A quick romp through the Bible, however, shows some problems with that idea. Let's start with Abraham, Sarah, and Sarah's slave Hagar to look at issues such as polygyny (and arguably polygamy and polyamory, not to mention the slavery and other abuses such as battery, attempted murder, and possibly pederasty) that challenge, in different ways, both the "biblical marriage" crowd's definitions and modern American categories of morality and consent.

38. See BBC, "The First Muslims in England" for a more in-depth look at the role of Muslims in sixteenth century England.

39. Winship, *Godly Republicanism*, 208.

theology with anyone who dared to take him on. The transcripts of his formal debates in 1672 with George Fox, founder of the Society of Friends, demonstrate how at the age of 73, he could still row approximately 25 miles from Providence to Newport and arrive full of vigor and ready for battle. Some historians note this debate represented one of the few times when Roger let his animosity towards another person's religious beliefs get the better of him. They do have a point here. The cordial tone he displayed even during his very public literary fights with John Cotton (the banisher of Anne Hutchinson and coiner of the term Congregationalism) appear to be noticeably absent from these proceedings. Given Roger accepted the challenge to debate Fox under duress by those politicos who wished to discredit the Quakers, perhaps the strain of entering into a fight he probably never wanted to start in the first place threw him a bit off guard. Then again, he really disliked the Quakers' beliefs.[40]

Roger disagreed vehemently with others about their belief systems, but he refused to exclude them from the full exercise of their right to practice said beliefs should they choose to become citizens of Rhode Island. Thus he created the American ideal of freedom of religion as a fundamental right. He welcomed those of other religions and even allowed atheists, agnostics, and heretics, outdoing later colonial founders like William Penn.[41]

Rhode Island's New England swampland became a haven for dissenters kicked out of England, the Massachusetts Bay Colony, and just about anywhere else. Even the Society of Friends could live here despite their tendency to quake at meetings and a belief in notions like universal salvation and the doctrine of perfection

---

40. Those looking for a more in-depth analysis of Roger's views on Quakerism can check out his book *George Fox Digged Out of His Burrowes*.

41. This is why Rhode Island became the home of Touro Synagogue, the first synagogue in the colonies. Also, I am calling the settlement founded by Roger "Rhode Island" for the sake of consistency even though some historians go with Providence Plantations and others use the phrase Colony of Rhode Island or Colony of Rhode Island and Providence Plantations. For more information about William Penn, see Public Broadcasting Service, "God In America."

that made Roger's skin crawl.⁴² In his daily life and governance, he lived out the motto that one can be neighborly without adopting a *Stepford Wives* type rigid conformity.⁴³

Just in case anyone feels Rhode Island's welcome to all meant Roger promoted a laid back "don't worry, be happy" kind of paradise, think again. Citizens may have gotten a reprieve from the religious persecution police, but they still were required to follow any civil laws on the books. Roger founded Rhode Island based on his belief that civil laws were necessary but needed to be kept separate from religious beliefs.

He railed against the very notion of a "Christian nation" on the grounds that those who call themselves Christians are bound to Christ by faith and repentance, not by government authority.⁴⁴ The founder of the first Baptist church in what later became the United States would be appalled at the sight of Jerry Falwell, Paul Pressler, and other Southern Baptists draping the cross of Christ with the American flag.⁴⁵ He could not for a nanosecond begin to comprehend their evangelical interpretation of a God who advances the notion of American exceptionalism while damning those to hell who do not follow in their way, truth, and light as anything other than political bullying masquerading as religion.⁴⁶

More to the point, this man brokered peace with Indigenous people and committed other acts of kindness that cannot be reconciled with a Lord and Savior who possessed a thirst for Old Testament style vengeance. No way would the creator of the first colonial

---

42. Hence the term "Quaker" which originally had pejorative connotations. See Friends General Conference, "FAQs about Quakers."

43. For Christianzed versions of this book, see Stepford Wives Organization and True Woman™. This first site is a joke (one would hope) but the second one is all too real.

44. Roger wrote that Constantine was a worse influence than Nero or Julian. See Williams, *The Bloudy Tenent,* 154–5, 316.

45. See Nelson, *Shadow Network* for an in-depth analysis of how Council for National Policy and the Southern Baptist Convention influenced US right wing politics.

46. For more information about this phrase see Walt, "The Myth of American Exceptionalism" and Zeitz, "Rethink American Exceptionalism."

charter granting religious liberty to all align himself with any Christian entity who sought to sit at the right hand of the President of the United States. Given the spirit of his 1644 masterpiece *The Bloudy Tenent of Persecution, for Cause of Conscience* where he rants about the evils of joining church and state together,[47] I strongly suspect Roger, rather than attending peaceably should anyone be so foolish as to give him a ticket, would sooner storm the halls of the National Prayer Breakfast. I envision him turning over the tables as Jesus of Nazareth is written to have done in the Temple and demanding that "Christian" leaders stop pushing the electorate to vote in their version of Americana Christianity.[48]

Rob Boston, Senior Policy Analyst for Americans United for the Separation of Church and State (AU), notes:

> Williams would strongly oppose those who seek to declare the United States an officially "Christian nation." Such a nation requires compulsion to exist, and Williams opposed coercion in matters of faith. This is the man, after all, who once proclaimed that "Forced religion stinks in the nostrils of God."
>
> In one of his most famous metaphors, Williams likens government to a ship at sea. The passengers are from many faiths, and what matters is not that the captain is of a particular faith but that he has the ability to pilot the vessel and maintain order. So it was with government. In Williams' view, the state should confine itself to keeping the peace among people and protecting them but not wade into theological controversies.

---

47. In penning this tome, Roger got into quite a row with fellow Puritan minister John Cotton. In response, Cotton penned *The Bloudy Tenent, Washed and Made White in the Bloud of the Lambe*. Roger then replied with *The Bloody Tenent Yet More Bloody: By Mr Cottons endevour to wash it white in the Blood of the Lambe*, a move that may have inspired fellow clergyman Jonathan Swift (1667–1745). Believe it or not, these two men remained cordial to each other on a personal level with Roger sounding even a bit affectionate towards Cotton.

48. Matthew 21:12–17, Mark 11:15–19, Luke 19:45–48, and John 2:13–22.

Williams understood that the notion of a "Christian nation" is not only nonsensical, it is impossible.[49]

50

Since the evangelical notion of a personal relationship with Jesus did not even come into play until the Second Great Awakening, Roger (and the Founding Fathers) would have no clue what accepting Jesus Christ as their personal Lord and Savior meant.[51] Revisionist pseudo-historians who pontificate how the U.S. of A. always possessed "Christian heritage" seem to have affixed on the Colonial American religious landscape their version of a fundamentalist faith that did not come into being until the post-Civil War Reconstruction era. Their interpretation of Jesus of Nazareth's teachings tend to be more Klan-informed than Christ inspired.[52]

Only the most brazen of pundits would attempt to ascertain what Roger's denominational preferences, if any, might be should he magically appear on earth today. Roger came to faith during an era when being a Puritan would be seen as taking a

49. Boston, E-mail.

50. Hayward, "Tell the Difference."

51. For an overview of how Jesus of Nazareth has been viewed throughout US history, see *American Jesus*—the book by Prothero, not the song by Bad Religion.

52. See Brown, "The Preacher Who Used Christianity."

countercultural stance against the crown; this is similar to someone professing to be an atheist, a Jew, or even an Episcopalian in parts of the Bible Belt today. Unlike seventeenth century dissidents, they might not get tortured and hung, but those sinners who fail to conform to the evangelical mindset can definitely feel like an outcast both personally and professionally.

We can infer from Roger's scandalous interactions with Indigenous people and radical welcome he extended to all that he would today still fight to ensure that everyone had the right to worship as they pleased.[53] Indeed, Roger even, unusually for the time and place, not only welcomed men of all religions, but also allowed women like Anne Hutchinson to exercise their freedom to preach, and supported a woman's right to exercise her own liberty of conscience, even against the wishes of her husband.[54]

Given Roger's desire to keep the church separate from the state, I could see him arguing against granting churches tax exemptions not available to secular nonprofit social service organizations. Using this same logic, I believe Roger would also require US citizens to pay their fair taxes as loyal subjects of the state. Given his striving for equality, I wonder how Roger would respond to the eighteenth century colonialists' cry of "no taxation without representation."[55] I suspect if he were subject to the unfair taxations forced upon eighteenth century colonists, he would be among those dumping tea and engaging in other acts of civil disobedience. Furthermore, he would probably be at the forefront today protesting federal funding for religious organizations, on the grounds that by accepting such monies, these entities will

---

53. Roger's use of the term "Indian" may have been deemed forward thinking within the context of a seventeenth century culture that deemed those living on the land they sought to colonize to be subhuman savages. I referenced the NAJA's guide "Reporting and Indigenous Terminology" as my guide in choosing to use the terms "Indigenous people" or "tribes."

54. "Roger Williams: The Verin Case" offers a succinct history of an instance where Roger supported a woman's right to worship with his community despite her husband's objections.

55. See Bell, "No Taxation Without Representation."

be required to adopt governmental policies that run counter to their religious beliefs.

Bill Leonard, founding dean of Wake Forest University, observes, "[Roger] anticipated American religious pluralism, even in ways that he himself would not have imagined at the time."[56] In the realm of democracy and civil rights, while Roger had wonderful thoughts on democracy, prefiguring Locke and Jefferson by decades, he wrote mainly on the freedom of religion.[57] He did not specifically address civil rights as we think of them now, such as the ability of those who were not white males of property to vote, or the civil status of non-Christians.[58]

For Roger, going against the established church meant not only identifying with the Puritan movement, but going further, disputing with those Puritan divines who wanted to purify the Church of England while still remaining on good graces with the crown. Today, he would be battling with a wider swath of Christian leaders including Pentecostals, Roman Catholics, and evangelicals, who each wish to craft their particular notions of God's will into laws that the entire populace must then follow.[59] Their motto seems to be "Religious liberty for me but not for thee."

Defining Religious Freedom

So, how does Rogers definition of "religious freedom" differ from the way this phrase is interpreted in twenty-first century US political circles? To Roger, religious freedom meant the right to practice your faith, or non-faith, unmolested by the government. Although much of the world tends to take this for granted today, in Roger's time the right to religious liberty was in no way secure. Monarchs

---

56. Garrison, "Soul Freedom versus Christian Nation."

57. See Barry, John M. "God, Government and Roger Williams."

58. See Panetta and Reaney, "The Evolution of American Voting Rights" and Morris, "Roger Williams and the Jews."

59. See Garrison, "Deconstructing Dominionism" for an analysis of the diversity within the twenty-first century socio-political religious landscape. *American Atheist*, 4th Quarter, 2011.

believed they had to align with a "true" faith and suppress other forms of religious expression that did not meet with their royal seal of approval.

What made Roger so radical is that he insisted the state was wrong to take sides on matters of faith. In doing so, he was essentially challenging the entirety of human history. It's even more startling when one considers that Roger advocated for the rights of people to worship in faiths he personally detested, such as the Quakers. He held a far-sighted vision of religious liberty that would greatly impact the American experience.[60]

Boston observes, "In our current discourse, too many people define 'religious liberty' as the right to run someone else's life and make decisions for them. Others assert that the government must 'help' religion by promulgating its doctrines, promoting its practice, displaying its symbols and awarding it tax support. If these things are not done, some argue, 'religious liberty' is not secure. This is a far cry from the ideal of religious liberty embraced by Williams."[61]

In defining his role in the public sphere, rather than creating Puritan enclaves designed to separate the saved from the damned or encouraging dialogue to "discuss" the rights of the "outsider," Roger chose to act. He employed his skills as a gifted linguist to embrace all, knowing we are not isolated individuals but part of a shared global humanity.[62]

So, what can we learn from this man who crafted the first state charter in the Western world that welcomed all religions? More to the point—in a pre-Enlightenment era, what was it in Roger's character that made him see the light a good fifty years before John Locke & Company, thus giving birth to the oldest charter of civil government in existence that granted religious liberty for all?

---

60. For a further historical examination of religious liberty see Bruckner and Bruckner, *In Freedom We Trust*.

61. Boston, E-mail.

62. Roger Williams knew at least seven languages: English, French, Latin, Dutch, Greek, Hebrew, and Narragansett. See National Park Service, "Frequently Asked Questions."

2
Piecing Together the Past

IN HIS SHORT BIOGRAPHY of Roger Williams, Edwin Gaustad observes how Roger (circa 1603–1683) presents a challenge for any biographer. "We do not know where he was born, nor exactly when he died. We do not know what he looked like. We cannot visit his home for it went up in flames long ago. Although he was a preacher, no sermon of his survives. During his lifetime, not a single monument was erected in his honor and, at his death no carved stone marked his grave. He was—or so it appeared—a forgotten man."[1]

---

1. Gaustad, *Roger Williams*, 7. The reference to flames might also encompass his sermons: Those works not burned by Parliament were destroyed in the Great Fire of London (1666) that devastated the city including Roger's childhood home. Also, I wonder what artifacts of his were destroyed when Providence went up in flames on March 29, 1676.

Roger's final resting place in Providence, RI[2]

Thanks to Gaustad, as well as a few other historians and biographers, I can piece together the existing shreds of Roger's rebel heritage.[3] These fragments help explain why his minority-of-one views continue to reverberate throughout the world.

   2. Those with an interest in forensic science might be intrigued by the escapades of Roger's body postmortem. See National Park Service, "The Tree Root That Ate Roger Williams."

   3. I crafted together the history of Roger's life and ministry thanks to these books: Arnold, *Rhode Island and Providence Plantations*; Barry, *Creation of the American Soul*; Carpenter, *Roger Williams: A Study*; Dexter, *Roger Williams and his Banishment*; Elton, *Life of Roger Williams*; Gaustad, *Roger Williams*; Knowles, *Memoir of Roger Williams*; Miller, *Roger Williams*; Straus, *Roger*

There are no birth records for Roger. One tradition states Roger was born in Wales. Historian James Knowles justifies this argument in part on the basis that Roger possessed the Welsh temperament— "excitable and ardent feelings, generosity, courage, and firmness, which sometimes, perhaps, had a touch of obstinacy."[4] Most historians though believe he was born in London, with the Roger Williams National Memorial website noting Roger was christened at St. Sepulcher Church in London.[5] Evidence indicates he spent his formative years in London, and his father James was a merchant tailor of some means who married a woman named Alice.

During his teens, Roger came to the attention of Sir Edward Coke, a brilliant jurist and one-time Chief Justice of England.[6] Apparently Coke was impressed by Roger's shorthand skills and utilized him as his transcriber. Under Coke's tutelage, Roger witnessed firsthand the troubles that could befall anyone who took a view contrary to the King of England and the Anglican Church.

Most historians do not believe Roger's father possessed the means or the social standing to procure a high caliber education for his son. But due to Coke's influence, Roger attended Charterhouse School in London and enrolled at Pembroke College in Cambridge where he graduated with honors.[7] A few historians note how his forcible and earnest writing belies his superior education. After Roger left England, he spent most of his life away from proper society leading an impoverished lifestyle. So it would stand to reason that his works never achieved the polished style that comes from conversing in sitting rooms and ivory towers instead of hanging with the riffraff of Rhode Island.

Upon graduation, Roger was ordained at the hands of an Anglican bishop. As was true of other Puritan divines, he adopted the Congregational mode of worship, which sought to "purify"

Williams; and Strickland, *Roger Williams*.

4. *Memoir of Roger Williams*, 23.

5. See National Park Service, "Roger Williams: Youth and Education."

6. See Barry, *Creation of the American Soul* for an in-depth analysis of Roger and Coke's relationship.

7. See "Roger Williams: Youth and Education."

Anglican services of their Catholic trappings. He became a private chaplain to Sir William Masham and his family. These English aristocrats defied the king, but they did so in the quiet privacy of their own homes. This allowed Roger a quiet observance of his faith, sheltered from the terror the state visited on those who professed Puritanism in public.

Following a crackdown in 1630 on all Puritan clergy, even private clergy, Roger set sail for the New World in search of religious tolerance, accompanied by his wife Mary. In the span of less than five years, Roger went from "godly minister" to solitary pilgrim.[8] He insisted on preaching the need to keep crown and church separate, and soon found himself on the outs with the Puritans of Boston, led by Winthrop. While he desired to "purify" the church from the more Catholic trappings of Anglicanism, Winthrop wanted to remain on good graces with the crown. Roger's integrity could never permit him to buy into that balancing act. They also disagreed over Winthrop's scriptural metaphors that employed biblical language to depict the Massachusetts Bay Colony as a Christian "City on a Hill," as noted previously.[9]

Every man over the age of 16 who resided in the colony was required to take the Freeman's Oath or face banishment. This oath changed the obligations of one's allegiance from the government of King Charles I to the Governor of the Massachusetts Bay Colony. However, Roger refused to take any oath that gave full authority to any earthly power.

The leaders of the Massachusetts Bay Colony accused him of maintaining the following dangerous opinions, among others: "First, That the magistrate ought not to punish the breach of the first table; otherwise than in such cases as did disturb the civil peace. Secondly, That he ought not to tender an oath to an unregenerate man. Thirdly, That a man ought not to pray with such, through wife, child, &c. Fourthly, That a man ought not to give thanks after the

---

8. "Godly minister" was the phrase cited by Winthrop upon welcoming Roger to Massachusetts Bay Colony. See "God In America."

9. See Matthew 5:14.

sacrament, nor after meat, &c."[10] Roger held that the state should not interfere with religious practices that do not break civil laws. Nor does the state have the right to require someone either to swear or to pray. This was all ultimately intolerable.

Once he got the boot from Boston, Roger sojourned in Salem and Plymouth. Here he continued to preach the separation of church and crown until 1635 when he was forced to flee from Salem, and indeed from all of Massachusetts, in the dead of winter. After settling in what is now called Rhode Island, Roger created a haven for those of any religious persuasion, including those who professed to have no faith. God-fearing Puritans would never dream of setting foot on soil populated by such unruly sorts. Derogatory terms such as "the sewer of New England," "the Licentious Republic," and "Rogues' Island" (or "Rouge Island") were used in reference to Roger's newfound homeland. If recent scandals are any indication, the tiniest state in the Union continues to live up to these nicknames.[11]

"Pulpit Rock: On this rock Roger Williams preached to the Indian inhabitants of Prudence Island"[12]

10 *Life of Roger Williams*, 29.
11. See Drogin. "'Rogues' Island' Lives Up to Nickname."
12. This rock and accompanying marker are located on the western side of

After establishing the first Baptist church in North America, Roger left this church after a few months. He never outlined the reasons for his departure except to note that with so many religious leaders clamoring to have the truth, he would have to just sit and wait for the new revelation to emerge. For the rest of his life, Roger still identified as a Christian, but of no particular denomination: friends and foes now called him a seeker.

In 1643, Roger began a battle with Parliament that eventually led to the creation of a charter for Rhode Island which made liberty of conscience a legal and binding principle throughout the entire colony. In addition to providing absolute protection for the right of conscience, this charter also became the first of its kind to acknowledge the rights of Indigenous people to own the titles to their own land.

Later, liberty of conscience became woven into the fabric of the First Amendment to the United States Constitution: "Congress shall make no law respecting an establishment of religion, or prohibiting the free exercise thereof."[13] From there, the principle spread throughout the modern world. Even though the Founding Fathers rendered religious liberty a constitutional right, throughout US history, Christians following in the Puritan mindset (aka the Winthrop Way) grant the right of religious liberty only to those churches and other religious entities that meet with their seal of approval. Not surprisingly, those deigned acceptable tend to be of the WASP variety. And of course, those drafting the Constitution failed to incorporate wording from the Rhode Island charter acknowledging the land rights of Indigenous people.

As I began to unpack these historical snippets, I seemed to have stumbled upon a most unusual character. According to Governor William Bradford of Plymouth Colony, Roger was "a man godly and zealous, having many precious parts."[14] Others have him of "no ordinary parts" with "a never-failing sweetness

---

Prudence Island, RI.

13. For commentary regarding how ideas originated by Roger made its way into the US Constitution, see Waldman's *Founding Faith*.

14. *Roger Williams and his Banishment*, 7.

of temper and unquestioned piety."[15] Even though Winthrop battled with Roger in public, their private correspondence reveals a lifelong genuine friendship. Despite all the wrongs done to him by Winthrop and others, Roger harbored no signs of desiring revenge. He kept his eyes on the prize, which for him meant securing the right for all to worship as they pleased. Historians bicker when putting together the fragments of Roger's life and ministry, but there appears to be a universal consensus that the ongoing success of Rhode Island's charter was due in large part to his soul and spirit.

> Williams was accused, even by those who loved him, of pride, of imperiousness, of conceit. Yet a student who applies himself to a close study of Williams' writing, though frequently irritated by his prolixity and pedantry, will soon come to know why even those who persecuted him had also to love him. To such a student Williams becomes most valuable—nay, truly invaluable—not merely because he propounded the idea of religious liberty to unheeding ears in America, but because underneath his arrogance lies a humility which true freedom begets.
>
> —Perry Miller[16]

Clearly he was a virtuous man whom even his enemies loved. What gleanings could we derive about his legacy that can help us live together in the public square in ways that can honor everyone? How does one try to enact social change without falling victim to the whims of partisan politics where one's vision becomes lost in a sea of compromises? What prevents a religious leader who knows in his heart he has found the truth from becoming so cocky and self-assured that he displays signs of arrogance and vanity fit for Narcissus? And on a more personal note, why did Roger not suffer a complete breakdown after a lifetime of banishment and rejection of his work, including the hardships he suffered during that winter flight?

---

15. Strickland, *Roger Williams*, 3.
16. Miller, "An Essay In Interpretation," 25.

Exploring the Virtues

In attempting to answer these questions, I asked my friends and peers for resources on the virtues, only to learn that I seemed to have stumbled upon a topic largely ignored by those living outside of the evangelical Christian bubble (aka in the real world). Somehow talking about "what it means to live a good life" has become the province of the religious right, used to impose their "biblically based" value system on the rest of us.

But why have we allowed this conversation about how we are to live together in the public square to be relegated to moralists like William J. Bennett? His fundamentalist rulebook views these virtues through a very strict black and white lens.[17] In this age of horizontal social media where we can all state our views in the public arena, what prevents us from standing up to these modern-day Goliaths and taking away their media megaphone?[18]

---

17. William Bennett's application of "biblical values" tends to work only for those who are white and male. They should also self identify as straight and be presentable enough that they can find a suitable Quiverfull woman to take as their godly wife. Ideally, she should possess the hair that praises Jesus and a personality befitting a 1 Peter woman who will remain biblically submissive to her earthly Lord and master. At a minimum, she cannot display any interest in working outside of the home and must be willing to repress her own sexual desires while making herself fully available to fulfill her husband's every need. (Exceptions can be made for the former in times of dire financial hardship provided she chooses a suitable position such as kindergarten teacher where her job remains clearly subordinate to that of her husband's career.)

Granted, most Christian couples cannot achieve the Duggar's level of 19 blessed children. (If somehow you missed out on the TLC reality TV show *19 Kids and Counting* that highlights the joys of Christian conception, consider yourself blessed.) But they will be required to keep trying sans contraception—God forbid they disobey his commandment to go forth and multiply as per Genesis 9:7. Should Satan prevent them from having any children on their own, these bible believers can adopt from a pre-approved list of missionary organizations that can help them find them a baby who has yet to hear about the love of Jesus.

18. Granted much of social media tends to be rubbish consisting of too many cute kitty YouTube videos, inane political ramblings from the latest reality celeb du jour, and smartphone pics of naked people that most of us would like our eyeballs back should we stumble upon them by accident. All too often, the material proves to be less than credible—mild understatement, too often

My few virtuous sources who studied this topic kept referring me back to the three big A's—Aristotle, Augustine, and Aquinas. Here one finds an admitted Western bias with Aristotle's conversations only including Athenian gentlemen. Slaves and women need not apply (despite that Aristotle's teacher, Plato, taught women, and his teacher, Socrates, was taught by one). Add to this mix centuries of debate among the myriad of philosophical and theological faith fights that transpired over the centuries, and soon I start humming Monty Python's "Bruces' Philosophers Drinking Song."[19]

Just because we cannot come to a uniform consensus regarding what it means to live a good life does not mean we should not try to explore this area. In this quest, I found a companion in the work of French philosopher André Comte-Sponville. As his book *The Little Book of Atheist Spirituality* resonated with my apophatic soul, I picked up his earlier work *A Small Treatise on the Great Virtues: The Uses of Philosophy in Everyday Life*. In this book, Comte-Sponville's

---

leading to hateful rhetoric, cyberbullying, and offline abuses.

But social media also told the stories of events like the Arab Spring and Occupy Wall Street, giving us fuller stories not told by traditional media outlets, as well as launching grassroots movements such as #metoo and its Christian equivalent #churchtoo. (Callahan, "#Metoo," Garrison, "#churchtoo," and Mak, "Occupy Wall Street.") With projects like "It Gets Better" and "I AM: Trans People Speak," social media can be employed to combat a deadly epidemic like anti-LGBTQ+ bullying and put a human face on marginalized communities. The problem isn't the tools themselves but the means by which they are employed, as well as the personalities of those who utilize these tools.

19. See Monty Python, "Bruces' Philosophers Song." For those unfamiliar, this recounts scandalous allegations pertaining to a number of world renowned philosophers with a particular focus on their ability (or lack thereof) to consume alcoholic beverages. I tend to leave the bar though once the boys start going all postmodern by flashing their Foucault, doing the Derrida dance, and getting all ziggy for Žižek. (For whatever reason, the Lacan-can-can never quite took off as a postmodern dance craze. Might be something to do with that whole showing off of one's panties dealie.) Next thing you know, the conversation devolves into a colossal whizzing contest. Women tend to be noticeably absent from these battles given we lack the necessary ontological equipment needed to engage in these type of missives. My further critique of postmodern/post-evangelical theology can be found in Garrison, *Jesus Died for This?*, 101–112.

analysis provided me with a practical guide to the gems inherent in over 2,500 years of classical teaching on this topic.

Comte-Sponville cites virtue as "an acquired and lasting way of being, it is what we are (and therefore what we can do), and what we are is what we have become."[20] Those who adhere to the Puritan way of being approach their faith from the belief that mankind exists within a binary good/evil dichotomy. This viewpoint tends to interpret one's individual faith journey through a black and white lens that deciphers those moral laws that must be followed in order to remain in God's good graces. Supposedly, those who play by the rules are guaranteed a place in the heavenly realm, though only the truly saved souls will receive the promise of placement at God's right hand.[21] In this worldview that focuses on the individual soul and not the good of the community, those who do not subscribe to their version of God get left behind.[22]

Like Roger and many other thinkers, Comte-Sponville rejects such a narrow interpretation of what it means to be a good person. Throughout the book, he raises some key questions: Who should we become? How do we relate to others? How are we to live our lives? In his search for answers, Comte-Sponville presents 18 virtues.

A quick review of select authors who have delved into this topic shows that the final list of virtues varies. While Plato may have written the oldest surviving list of the four virtues—prudence, temperance, justice, and courage—Aristotle's presentation

---

20. Comte-Sponville, *A Small Treatise*, 3.

21. Of course, no one has yet come back from the great beyond to inform us who among the elect actually made it through the very narrow Pearly Gates. Furthermore, no one can say for certain the exact persons who got invited to sit at God's right hand, not to mention who received the finger instead of the whole hand due to some minor theological technicality. This raises the whole question as to whether or not any being who exists outside of time and space even has hands let alone a physical body. Then again, I cannot fathom why any Father worthy of worship would be obsessed with the grand heavenly seating chart and "personal sins" like masturbation, yet not intervene directly to prevent genocide and other unspeakable horrors. But I digress.

22. Though one hopes that regardless of our fallen state, we might get spared from the hell of being featured in any Armageddon themed movie. That would be godawful indeed.

of these virtues is perhaps better known.[23] They represent the fundamentals on which hinge what constitutes a good person.

By the time of St. Augustine, they were called the cardinal virtues, from the Latin word "cardo" which means hinge or astronomical pole. The early Church Fathers added three theological virtues (faith, hope, and charity) but this latter trio was only applicable to those who chose to follow the Christian faith. As those who ruminate about sin and such are wont to do, shortly thereafter a list of dos and don'ts became crafted into a set of seven virtues (chastity, temperance, charity, diligence, patience, kindness, and humility) along with seven deadly sins (wrath, greed, sloth, pride, lust, envy, and gluttony) that represent the mirror opposites of these virtues.[24] Later virtue list makers included Benjamin Franklin, who compiled 13 virtues, and Bennett, who claims 10 "Christian" virtues.[25] As previously noted, Comte-Sponville tops the list with 18 virtues.[26] While I admire these more extensive lists, applying Roger's life to each of these virtues would transform this short book into a lengthy tome designed primarily for insomniacs.

---

23. See Plato, *Republic* 427e, 435a-b.

24. According to an e-mail exchange with the Rev. Kurt Neilson, author of *Urban Iona*, Evagrius of Pontus (345–399 CE) compiled a work from which were derived in part the "seven deadly sins." For Evagrius and the desert mothers and fathers, such an identification was diagnostic of diseases of the soul, and the "remedy" was the application of the corresponding virtue—patience for wrath, for example. Later church teachings transformed this diagnostic model into a punitive one replete with a set of prescribed steps that all virtuous people must follow, lest they succumb to the vices and be damned to a life of eternal hellfire. Also, with regards to chastity, as evidenced by the countless little cardinals running around the Vatican at various points throughout history, the more contemporary priestly pedophilia scandals, and the number of Catholic monks and priests with "special friends," chastity never seemed to be one of these dudes' strong suits from the get-go. However, it must be noted that originally this meant only the decision to not marry, which was at least as much about passage of property rights as anything else, rather than to not have sex.

25. See Eliot, ed. *The Autobiography of Benjamin Franklin*, 79–80 and Bennett, *The Book of Virtues*, Table of Contents.

26. See *A Small Treatise*, ix-x.

Roger and the Four Cardinal Virtues

I settled on applying the four cardinal virtues to Roger's life, as they were the ones that kept emerging as having an almost universal consensus regardless of one's particular belief system.[27] Also, Roger was doubtless exposed to the cardinal virtues and their applications during his classical education.

One can clearly see Roger's courage and drive for justice in his ongoing defiance of unjust governance. However, prudence and temperance do not immediately seem like words one would ever use to describe Roger. After all, this is a man who described the act of forcing someone to go against their conscience as "soul rape."[28] And he paid for his blunt and forcible language. Besides his exile, the House of Commons burned his masterpiece, *The Bloudy Tenent of Persecution, for Cause of Conscience*. In this book, he describes a host of vile acts committed by religious authorities at the behest of the crown.

Roger's colleague John Milton published the *Areopagitica*, his plea for religious toleration, the same year Roger got all Bloudy in public. These two friends were cut from the same intellectual cloth with Roger teaching Milton Dutch in exchange for Milton tutoring him in other languages.[29] But Milton's commentary was far more tempered, as he stressed the need for all to live together in harmony without demanding the individual right of soul liberty.

If Roger had played his hand a bit more deftly, could he have ended up with the same legacy as Milton? Had he stayed in England after securing a charter for Rhode Island, might the name "Roger Williams" be featured more prominently in the history

---

27. The notable exception would be the virtue 'n' vice crew who would undoubtedly reject any list that didn't provide them with the means to condemn the unwashed masses. Roger's personal life suggests that while he adopted a life designed to keep the seven vices at bay, he rejected those who insisted that all must follow such a strict rule of life. Having said that, he required that people follow civil laws in order to ensure the common good.

28. Williams, *The Bloudy Tenent*, 187.

29. Elton, *Life of Roger Williams*, 104.

books? In addition to conversing in multiple languages with Milton, he also entertained conversations with Oliver Cromwell.[30] By this time, the Puritan elites were no longer locked up in the Tower of London or executed, so one could now be a Puritan minister and still live a gentlemanly life.

Following intermittent battles with poor health that drained him physically, though his mind retained its sharp agility, Roger died in 1683 with his books burned and his reputation tarnished. His legacy took another hit in 1702 when Puritan minister Cotton Mather, grandson of John Cotton, penned a book that painted Roger as a dangerous revolutionary. This move continued to keep Roger's name out of the history books. I doubt his works graced the libraries of the Founding Fathers, given they do not reference him in their voluminous writings.

In 1777, Isaac Backus wrote a book titled *A History of New England with particular reference to the denomination of Christians called Baptists* that partially redeemed Roger, but he remained a largely forgotten figure in the fight for religious liberty. His banishment from the Massachusetts Bay Colony remained in effect until the Massachusetts House passed Bill 488 in 1936 that rescinded his expulsion, thus ending over 300 years of exile.[31] A trek around Massachusetts yields few remembrances of Roger: a plaque at the house where he might have resided at Salem, the First Parish Church in Plymouth noting the years he served this church, and a few other very minor signs that "Roger was here."

This man whose most noble feature was a steadfast love of truth might have been too hasty and rash in forming his opinions, as well as unwilling to compromise. Bernard Bailyn noted in *The Barbarous*

---

30. Some historians have tried to prove that Roger Williams is a relative of Oliver Cromwell but the lineage linking him to Cromwell's line seems a bit sketchy. However, Roger was apparently on a first-name basis with Cromwell, which implies a possible familial relationship. Still, I'm not going to start calling the Lord Protector, "Oliver."

31. See Goddard, "Roger Williams: Champion of Liberty." In the same year Roger got un-banished from Massachusetts, the state of Rhode Island issued a 3 cent stamp bearing his likeness. For a depiction of this stamp, see US Postage Stamps, "Roger Williams 1936."

Years that "while Williams—sympathetic to the Indians' civility, ruthlessly logical, incapable of compromise with his vision of the primitive church—was forever the subject of bitter condemnation, he was always personally respected."[32] Roger possessed a benevolent and magnanimous spirit that drew people towards him personally even after many people he called friends expelled him from their company. Upon further exploration, I realized his ability to live out these four virtues prevented him from becoming yet another itinerant preacher ranting away on some street corner.

Unlike Aristotle, Augustine, and Aquinas, Roger didn't tackle the virtues directly. But we can explore how through the diligent application of prudence and temperance, Roger was able to employ the virtues of justice and courage to craft a charter that would define "religious liberty" for everyone (including non-Christians) and that continues to stand the test of time.

---

32. Bailyn, *The Barbarous Years*, 434.

3
Prudence

FOR ME, PRUDENCE REPRESENTS an island in Narragansett Bay that saved my sanity.[1] No matter how horrid things got with my alcohol riddled family, I could always retreat back to Prudence Island, Rhode Island. Reflect at Pulpit Rock where Roger preached to the Narragansett tribe, as well as sit by Narragansett Bay. Even when I was a small child, the waves told me somehow I would get through whatever calamity lay in front of me. Recently I have come to fancy that what I heard were Roger's words echoing in my ears every time the waves hit the rocks.[2]

    1. From what little information I can find, Roger would venture over to Prudence Island to restore his soul as well. For more information about Prudence, as well as neighboring Patience, Hope, and Hog islands, see *Rhode Island and Providence Plantations*, 105. As Roger never discussed why he gave these islands these names, we cannot conclude if he named the first three after the virtues or not.
    Family story: Roger really wanted a boy. So when Mary had a baby girl, he named her Prudence because he knew he needed to be prudent in waiting for a male heir. When the second baby was born and it was again a girl, Roger named the baby Hope as he was still hoping for a boy. When their third child turned out to also be a girl, Roger named the baby Patience, as he was losing his patience. Finally, the fourth baby was born and finally a boy. However, this baby proved to be a very voracious eater, and so they named the boy Hog. And the islands are named after the children.
    Reality: Roger and Mary had six children, four girls, Mary, Freeborn, Providence, and Mercy, and two boys, Joseph and Daniel. So maybe one child was named after a Rhode Island town.
    2. I recounted how the Narragansett Bay saved me in an improvisational piece titled "Water Talk" that I did under the auspices of the late Gary Austin, founder of The Groundlings. Portions of this were reprinted in Garrison, *The*

Likewise, this cardinal virtue became the glue that allowed Roger to remain relevant centuries later instead of being conscripted to the dustbins of history. Comte-Sponville describes prudence as the disposition that makes it possible to deliberate correctly on what is good or bad for man (not in itself but in the world as it is, and not in general but in specific situations), and through such deliberation to act appropriately. "Prudence is what differentiates action from impulse and heroes from hotheads."[3]

We have virtually no information about Roger's political or religious involvements prior to his ordination. He angered his father when he became a Puritan, though not to the extent that his father disowned him. In fact, numerous accounts indicate Roger received an inheritance from his father's estate. Coke, Roger's mentor, might have been a bit of a rebel but given his proximity to King James I, he could not permit a loose cannon to accompany him to court. Specifically, he never would have entrusted anyone to transcribe some very explosive and life altering legal battles unless he was certain this scribe could keep himself composed at all times. In a similar vein, Coke would need to be certain he could trust this person not to forward any material of a confidential nature to the Puritan mob, where these papers would only add more fuel to the battles waging throughout England and Continental Europe, nor to the King's secret police. Clearly, Roger showed discretion at an early age.

As he matured, Roger managed to keep whatever unease he felt at bay so he could complete his schooling at Charterhouse and Pembroke College. Then again, history books don't record any demonstrations among seventeenth century students attending either school. So one wonders if Roger would have joined in with his fellow young idealists had the opportunity presented itself.

The scant surviving evidence suggests he was introduced to Congregationalist principles not from studying the tomes of respected ministers like William Ames but from the English Puritan sectarian underground, the London Jacob congregationalist

---

New Atheist Crusaders, 134–135.

3. *A Small Treatise*, 34.

church, and perhaps the General Baptist offshoots of the Barrow separatists.[4] In other words, on occasion, he ran with a bit of a rough rebel crowd, those voted most likely to get tortured.

Roger emerged from these lowly associations unscathed for his name does not appear in historical accounts of the more radical populist wing of those railing against the crown. Somehow he remained prudent enough to utilize those connections he made via Coke so he could navigate this world without becoming yet another tortured casualty. Given the lack of any concrete evidence regarding Roger's life during this time period, how he kept himself alive while defying the crown remains pure speculation.

The first major outward sign that Roger could apply the virtue of prudence with success occurred after he became a chaplain to Sir William Masham of Otes in the parish of High Laver, Essex. By all accounts, his extensive knowledge of history and theology, as well as his scholarship in classic languages, made him a valuable asset to this household. Even though Archbishop William Laud had already begun to persecute Puritan chaplains, initially he left those clerics alone who served in private homes. When Laud began to put some pressure on private chaplains, Sir William's social standing initially kept ecclesiological stormtroopers from invading his estate.

In April 1629, Roger asked Lady Jane Barrington for permission to marry her niece Jane Whalley. Apparently Roger and Jane had fallen in love and begun a covert relationship of sorts. Roger's friend Roger Masham was the son of Sir William Masham and also the son-in-law to Lady Jane Barrington. Given this connection, Roger hoped Lady Barrington might permit them to marry despite the glaring fact that his social status in seventeenth century England rendered him unworthy to assume the position of husband to a titled woman. Lady Barrington, whose social connections included her nephew Oliver Cromwell, agreed with Roger's assessment that he was unworthy for such a position.

---

4. See Winship, *Godly Republicanism,* 208. The exact years when Roger hung out with this crew are not known though one can presume he would be at least aware of their existence by the time he was ordained.

Apparently Roger fell deathly ill upon receiving the news that he could not marry his true love. Some historians state he was nursed back to health by Mary Barnard, a maid to Lady Masham's daughter, though there is no documented evidence to support this claim. Roger never mentions if he met Mary prior to his illness, though the estate was small enough that those employed by Sir Masham would know each other at least by face. Hence, one can feel fairly certain that Mary had an inkling about Roger's passionate wooing of Lady Jane before he settled for her. I wonder how she felt about being seen as the runner up for his affections. Did she fear she would be a maid forever in more ways than one if she said, "No?"

To be clear, Mary functioned as a companion or a lady-in-waiting, not a member of the cleaning crew. In this capacity, she would have acquired the necessary graces to make her a suitable minister's wife especially since her father, the Rev. Richard Barnard, was in the same profession as Roger. Since Roger never mentions the Rev. Barnard in his correspondence, we cannot ascertain the extent of his relationship with his father-in-law.

By now he was in his late twenties, and if Roger wanted a substantial career, then he needed to secure a suitable wife.[5] Mary fit the bill. After recovering from a broken heart, Roger apparently set his mind to fulfill his role as a proper vicar, and married Mary on December 15, 1629. His later correspondence to Mary never indicated the degree of passion he is reputed to have felt towards Lady Barrington's niece, though he does express affection for Mary as a lifelong companion. While I can feel some sympathy for Roger's predicament and Mary's possible unease over this entire situation,

---

5. This pressure to present oneself as a traditional married couple in order to secure employment continues to this day in too many church contexts. Even in somewhat more progressive evangelical/emergent settings, pastors and youth ministers are expected to arrive with spouse in hand and preferably children in tow. These Christians tend to rush into early marriages in order to avoid committing the forbidden sin of premarital sex. One can speculate to what extent this expectation to conform to the "happy-happy-joy-joy" Christian family leads to sexual dysfunction and divorce down the road by those who felt compelled to marry at such an early age. This is especially true for those believers who know in their soul, or later discover, they are gay, lesbian, or bisexual.

had he been permitted to marry his true love, I wouldn't be here. So out of concerns for my own self-interest and preservation, I am pleased that he married my 12th-great-grandmother.

This incident of wooing a woman well beyond his means marked the last time Roger ever did anything that seemingly would give him preference or personal advancement. Perhaps he realized he could not live in the moment by seeking out his own desires with scant regard for his future. As much as he might desire Lady Barrington's niece, he could not always take the shortest route to pleasure. As Comte-Sponville noted, "Reality imposes its laws, its obstacles, its detours. Prudence is the art of taking them into account; it is lucid and reasonable desire.[6]

Shortly following this rejection and his subsequent marriage, we see how Roger put this principle into practice. Following his request to marry the niece of Lady Barrington, Roger discovered his services were no longer required by the Masham family. The exact reasons for Roger's dismissal were never made explicit, though one can presume that Lady Barrington made her displeasure known to Sir Masham. Also, by this time Laud was putting the screws, sometimes literally, on all dissenting clergy. Ministers more moderate than Roger lost their living, were imprisoned, and in some cases killed.[7]

Another man might have gone back to Coke and sought out his favor to secure another appointment, even though such an encounter would almost undoubtedly have placed Coke's social standing in jeopardy. At this juncture, odds are anyone meeting with a rebel Puritan minister would face at the very least a fine that would render them bankrupt. With no sign of Laud relaxing his grip on private chaplains, even someone of Coke's stature might not be able to protect Roger anyway. Those Puritan chaplains not willing to recant their views faced an almost certain imprisonment at best should they decide to remain in England. Given his current unemployed status and apparent possession of radical views even

---

6. *A Small Treatise*, 34.

7. In a bit of karmic justice, Laud was later executed for his persecution of Puritans. See Encyclopedia Britannica, "William Laud."

more extreme than those of his peers, Roger must have realized he needed to join his fellow Puritans in the Massachusetts Bay Colony immediately. His later correspondence indicates a profound sadness for not being able to inform Coke of this journey, though Roger indicated that knowledge of his whereabouts could endanger his mentor's well-being. So, despite his personal desire to say his goodbyes, he chose the more prudent path by deciding to set sail without paying Coke a visit.

Roger embarked from Bristol on the ship *Lyon* accompanied by his wife. After arriving in Boston on February 5, 1631, he was offered the position of minister for First Church in Boston as the current minister had returned to England for a spell. Serving as an upstanding Puritan minister would have secured a comfortable life for his wife and eventual family. But Roger lacked a self-serving gene and refused to pastor this church or any other church that remained beholden to the crown.

Putting Prudence Into Practice

Prudence Island, RI at Sunset

Throughout his ministry, Roger put into practice Comte-Sponville's explanation of how "prudence represents a virtue only when it is in the service of honorable ends (otherwise it amounts to shrewdness) and, by the same token, ends are entirely virtuous only when served by adequate means (otherwise they would amount to worthy sentiments)."[8] He demonstrated his steadfast desire to seek out that which is honorable by putting the values of religious liberty ahead of his own personal comfort. This desire to follow one's conscience was not intended for his own personal gain, for him alone to do as he pleased, but as a freedom for the betterment of all.

In lieu of damning those who sent him out into the wilds in the dead of winter, Roger chose to be grateful for the assistance provided to him by the local tribes who gave him shelter and sustenance. He did not bemoan how this experience made him deathly ill for the second time in his life. Instead, he named the city he founded Providence based on the belief that God sustained him and his followers and brought him to this providential land.

While other settlers took the land they desired, Roger believed this land belonged to those Indigenous people already living there when the colonists arrived. He used his skills as a linguist to learn their language, and he negotiated with them to secure land grants with terms favorable to both parties. These close relationships not only sustained him during his banishment, but also made possible the settlement of a swath of land deemed desolate and uninhabitable but for "savages."[9]

In 1636, some members of the Pequot tribe attacked a sloop near Block Island, Rhode Island and murdered John Oldham, who was one of the traders.[10] Roger caught wind that the tribes had

---

8. *A Small Treatise*, 35.

9. If anyone witnessed the antics of some of my fellow Williams relatives especially when alcohol enters the picture, they just might question just how civilized bits of Rhode Island are even today.

10. Oldham was so beloved by the Narragansett tribe that they gave him the island of Chibachuweset which Roger later renamed Prudence Island. Upon Oldham's death, Roger could have asserted his right to Oldham's property. Instead, he purchased this island from the Narragansett tribe.

begun to coalesce with the intention of annihilating all the existing colonies. By this time, he had established enough friendships among the Narragansett tribe that he could negotiate with them to secure his personal safety and keep his family free from harm. My strong hunch is that when put into this position, most people would not concern themselves one whit with the welfare of those who drove them from their home. Odds are their response would range from "serves you right" to benign indifference.

Roger adopted a more prudent approach. He not only warned the governor of Massachusetts about the possibility of war, but also negotiated with the Narragansett tribal leaders, as well as ambassadors from the warring Pequot tribe, to break this league. Over the next year, as the Pequots continued to fight, Roger served as an adviser to prevent these skirmishes from developing into a full blown war. Later, his prudent behavior was amply rewarded, for when these wars reached their bloodiest and even Providence got more than a bit singed, the Narragansett tribal leaders informed Roger they would spare him and his family due to his years of kindness towards them.

Despite these overtures that saved Massachusetts from annihilation, the Massachusetts Bay Colony leaders still refused to let Roger enter the holier than thou colony. An incident involving the Rev. John Clarke, Obadiah Holmes, and John Crandall, then of Newport, Rhode Island, demonstrates just how far these leaders would go in order to suppress liberty of conscience. These men were appointed by the Rhode Island Colony to visit William Witter of Lyme, Massachusetts. On account of his age, he had requested a visit from his brethren. As part of this visit, Clarke preached on Sabbath at the house. The three were arrested and imprisoned for charges related to preaching without permission. Without Clarke's knowledge, someone paid his fine, so Crandall and he were released, though Holmes refused to pay the fine and received a good whipping.[11]

---

11. See New England Historical Society, "Obadiah Holmes, The Baptist Martyr."

Rhode Island residents could not even obtain arms and ammunition to defend themselves. In a similar vein, this colony was not invited to be part of the United Colonies of New England (also known as the New England Federation) formed to protect the colonies from further attacks. The other New Englanders seemed to forget that without Roger's negotiation skills, they all might have gone the way of the Lost Colony of Roanoke. In *The Wordy Shipmates*, Sarah Vowell reflects, "Roger Williams's heretical colony is purposefully left out of the coalition so Rhode Island's anything-goes cooties won't rub off on its proper God-fearing neighbors."[12]

Later when Roger journeyed to England to secure the first charter, he could not sail out of Boston Harbor but had to make the lengthy trek to New York Harbor. The Dutch, who were more commercially minded, welcomed Roger, especially after he assisted them with their problems with the local tribes on Long Island following the murder of Anne Hutchinson.[13]

Instead of letting these slights fester, Roger chose to reflect on how "Rhode Island (i.e., Aquidneck) was obtained by love . . . and favor which that honorable gentleman, Sir Henry Vane, and myself, had with that great sachem, Miantonomo, about the league which I procured between the Massachusetts English and the Narragansetts in the Pequot War."[14]

For once, history appeared to be on Roger's side. Historians speculate that his close relationship with Vane contributed greatly to the British Parliament granting Roger a charter for Rhode Island in 1644. After Vane replaced Winthrop as Governor of the

---

12. Vowell, *The Wordy Shipmates*, 35.

13. After moving to Portsmouth, Rhode Island, Anne Hutchinson and her family enjoyed a relatively quiet existence. After the death of her husband in 1642, she moved with her family to New York. There she along with five of her youngest children were murdered by local tribes with a daughter taken into captivity. The next time you find yourself stuck on the Hutchinson River Parkway trying to get out of New York City, think of how bad poor Anne had it. Kind of helps to put things into perspective doesn't it? See New World Encyclopedia, "Anne Hutchinson."

14. King, *Sir Henry Vane, Jr.*, 65. Sachem is the modern English for the Narragansett word. See Williams, *Key to the Language*, 132.

Massachusetts Bay Colony, the two men became good friends. Vane remained governor until he sided with Anne Hutchinson when she was put on trial for disrupting the colony with her scandalous preaching.[15] After Winthrop's son John Winthrop Jr. won this battle, Vane got so disgusted that he returned to England where he lived out the rest of his life.

Rhode Island may have developed a reputation as a haven for outcasts, but that doesn't mean the state became this unified Oz-like paradise of religious liberty free from any and all conflict. Some cranks who resided in the colony took advantage of Roger's good nature.[16] They viewed liberty as a license to disregard any legal regulations that might be imposed upon them by the colony. Their anarchist leanings failed to distinguish between the need to impose some limits on personal liberty to ensure the general welfare of all and restrictions imposed by tyranny.[17]

After the execution of Charles I in 1649, William Coddington, an early magistrate of the Massachusetts Bay Colony and later Rhode Island, got Parliament to give him lifelong political control over much of Rhode Island.[18] In response, a number of colonists asked John Clarke to go to England along with Roger and confirm the original charter obtained by Roger. (Yes, this is the same Clarke who was fined for preaching in Massachusetts.)[19]. After Roger and Clarke restored the charter rather quickly, Roger stayed in England until 1654. When he returned back to Rhode Island, he came alone and Clarke stayed on the other side of the pond.

---

15. See Constitution Society, "Examination of Mrs. Anne Hutchinson."

16. Take for instance Samuel Gorton, a class A crackpot if there ever was one. For a sampling of his antics, check out Straus, *Roger Williams*, 146–153.

17. In his "Letter to the Town of Providence," Roger sought to quell dissent by once again reiterating his clarion call of religious liberty for papists and protestants, Jews, and Turks. In this brief letter, he makes it clear that should those mutiny, the commander or commanders may judge, resist, compel obedience against, and punish such transgressors.

18. Encyclopedia Britannica, "William Coddington."

19. For a more detailed history of Clarke's life and work, see James, "John Clarke and His Legacies."

Back in Rhode Island, devout Anglicans complained of Roger's religious separatism to Oliver Cromwell. The Lord Protector directed them to the charter which granted religious liberty to any resident of Rhode Island. A letter from Roger's friend Vane, who by now was serving as part of Cromwell's crew, helped quell divisions within the colony.[20]

Roger's leadership hit another crisis point once King Charles II assumed the throne in 1660 and executed Cromwell's cronies, including Vane. Cromwell would have been included in this mix except he died in 1658 and received a state funeral. Once King Charles II came into power, Cromwell's body was exhumed and his corpse hung in full public view. After his body was taken down from the gallows, his head got severed with eight blows. Then his head was placed on a 20-foot pole and raised above Westminster Hall.[21] No communication exists from Roger regarding this incident but he had to know that the charter he secured under the rule of Oliver Cromwell was now null and void.

One could easily question why Charles II did not simply order Clarke to be killed, tortured, or at the very least imprisoned in the tower. The term "at the very least" is applied here rather ironically. Due to diseases and harsh treatment of the prisoners, being sent to the Tower of London would be akin to a death sentence unless one received a rather quick pardon from the king. However, Charles had issued a statement of political amnesty and religious toleration before being crowned, the Declaration of Breda, and he apparently meant to live by it.

This second charter for Rhode Island that Clarke eventually secured in 1663 deemed the colony to be a "lively experiment" whereby the civil state could furnish the colonists with full liberty in religious concerns. According to this new law of the land:

> That our royal will and pleasure is, that no person within the said colony, at any time hereafter, shall be anyway

---

20. For a more detailed background on Vane's life and work, see *Sir Henry Vane, Jr.*

21. See *The Wordy Shipmates*, 118–122 for a more in-depth take on Cromwell's corpse.

molested, punished, disquieted, or called in question, for any differences in opinion in matters of religion, and does not actually disturb the civil peace of our said colony; but that all and every person and persons may, from time to time, and at all times hereafter, freely and fully have and enjoy his and their own judgments and consciences, in matters of religious concernments, throughout the tract of land hereafter mentioned; they behaving themselves peaceably and quietly, and not using this liberty to licentiousness and profaneness, nor to the civil injure or outward disturbance of others; any law, statute, or clause, therein contained, or to be contained, usage or custom of this realm, to the contrary hereof, in any wise, notwithstanding.[22]

Thanks in large part to Roger's powers of persuasion and Clarke's persistence, the English nobility decided to go along with this lively experiment. Some historians speculate that as these noblemen perceived the inhabitants of this swamp land to be uncivilized, they felt confident in granting permission for a mission they felt would fail. In other words, let them have their charter and play this little liberty of conscience game. Once the colony was annihilated, the British nobles could then claim that religious freedom cannot succeed without the oversight afforded by the crown. Then maybe they could get back to their bible business as usual by employing religion as a tool to control and oppress those under the control of the crown.[23]

Fortunately, Roger kept these glaring slights from getting the better of him. The more I reflect on the gaslighting in the name of God that he got from his more rabid critics like John Cotton and his descendants, the easier it becomes for me to laugh when a few free range theologians respond to my critiques of their work by calling me names like troll, hack, liar, mean, poisonous source, mental, wingnut, and my favorite slam "Hitler."[24] Unlike Roger

22. See Rhode Island, "Charter of Rhode Island"

23. See *Rhode Island and Providence Plantations*, 291–386 for the full history of Coddington and Clarke's roles in this charter debate.

24. For one to be called Hitler doesn't that entail that in order for one to

who almost always managed to keep his cool, I can let my anger get the better of me at times if I'm not careful.[25]

Roger succeeded under grueling circumstances. Most men would have been borne down by the opposition or abandoned any hope of reconciliation due to the narrow views of some individuals, even in supposedly liberal Rhode Island. Because he proved to be far more prudent than most, we now have freedom of religion entrenched firmly in place in the US Constitution, with similar wording in the United Nations Declaration of Human Rights and in many countries around the world. In theory, the First Amendment grants all US citizens the right to worship as we please as long as we accord others the same freedom by putting into practice the late comedian George Carlin's favorite commandment: "Thou shalt keep thy religion to thyself.[26]

> I ask, whether or no such as may hold forth other worships or religions, Jews, Turks, or anti-christians, may not be peaceable and quiet subjects, loving and helpful neighbors, fair and just dealers, true and loyal to the civil government? It is clear they may, from all reason and experience in many flourishing cities and kingdoms of the world.
>
> —ROGER WILLIAMS, *The Bloudy Tenent of Persecution, for Cause of Conscience*[27]

---

follow lockstep in the Fuhrer's footsteps, one must possess only one testicle? Using that logic wouldn't that rule out all who were born genetically female, as well as men who have all their bits intact? Then again, those who fulfill Godwin's Law aren't exactly noted for conducting sane and reasoned debates. The law was promulgated by Mike Godwin in 1990, who explains the origins of this meme in "Meme, Counter-meme."

25. My reflections on trying to hold myself accountable for my actions and attempt reconciliation when possible were posted on the God's Politics blog, "Experiments in Accountability."

26. Carlin, "Why We Don't Need 10 Commandments."

27. Williams, *The Bloudy Tenent*, 112–113.

Paper mâché statue of Roger (1960)[28]

28. According to the sign tacked to the back of this paper mâché likeness currently housed at the Roger Williams National Memorial, this artifact was commissioned in 1960 by officials of the Roger Williams Savings and Loan Association. Because no accurate likeness of Roger exists, creators of the statue had to make an educated guess as to Williams's features. It stands 7-feet tall and weighs 170 pounds. See National Park Service, "Liberty of Conscience."

4
Justice

WHILE GROWING UP NEAR the Smithfield plain in London, an area with a bloody history, Roger may have seen Bartholomew Legate being burned at the stake for heresy.[1] While others gloated at the sight, or simply walked on by seemingly oblivious to the cries and the obvious stench emanating from the gruesome scene, Roger's vehement opposition to persecuting people for their religious beliefs may have been influenced by this childhood memory. He never discussed his parents' reactions to this site's infamous history. One can presume they were among the vast majority of Londoners who simply looked the other way and went about their business.

But Roger seems to have been born with an innate sense of justice. Since we cannot trace his family history back any further than his father, we have no way of knowing if justice might have been grafted into his DNA. But somehow, he knew he could not align himself with the Anglican Church given their role in perpetuating such atrocities. So at the age of 11, he declared himself to be a Puritan, who at this time were among the religious minorities being persecuted by the crown. (This was well before the Puritans moved to the Massachusetts Bay Colony and went from being persecuted by the crown for not following the Anglican state religion to persecuting others for not following the Puritan faith. The careful

---

1. For a brief history of Legate's fate see Past Tense, "Bartholomew Legate Burnt for Heresy." Some historians think Roger grew up in the neighboring section of Holburn instead. If that is true, then it's unlikely he would have witnessed this execution or its aftermath. For more on the history of Smithfield, see Marxists, "The Peasants' Revolt. 1381."

reader and parishioner might have seen or heard signs of what was to come.) As Roger never explained in any of his writings why he made this monumental decision, we can only speculate as to why he rejected the Anglicanism of his early childhood.

Comte-Sponville observes how, "Of the four cardinal virtues, justice is probably the only one that is an absolute good in itself. Prudence, temperance, and courage are virtues only when they serve good ends, either directly or else by furthering other virtues—justice for example—that transcend them or motive them. Prudence, temperance, and courage in the service of evil or injustice would not be virtues, merely talents or qualities of mind or temperament."[2]

As I've learned in my years reporting on the rise and fall of celebrities, you really don't know a person's character until you see how they respond when given a bit of power and put into the spotlight.[3] Will they use their new-found street cred to build up the neighborhood for the good of all? Or will they utilize whatever slivers of fame come their way to build up their own Napoleonic kingdom? My experience covering Americana Christianity since 1994 tells me that when given the opportunity, most leaders will choose the latter course of action. As much as they want to "do good," their natural instinct for self-preservation coupled with any underlying narcissistic qualities will rise to the forefront whenever anyone dares threaten whatever fiefdom they have created.[4] Like

---

2. *A Small Treatise*, 61.

3. I've lost track by now of the promising new voices I helped promote who became all American Idol-ized once they scored a book deal, and then allowed themselves to be pigeonholed and marketed via the latest "hot" branded publishing platform. Some potential labels include: armchair activist, a/theist, Christian atheist, cussin' pastor, emergent/emerging, ex-evangelical, holy hipster, Jesus follower, missional, new monastic, organic, post-church, post-liberal, postmodern, progressive, slow church, tattooed theologian, and the list goes on and on and on.

4. I strongly suspect there's a preponderance of narcissists with a surprising number of these souls also possessing psychopathic/sociopathic tendencies among those who brand themselves as Christian author/speakers. Yes, one finds egos in every profession especially in those fields that elevate a select few to the spotlight. But only in the Christian publishing world do you

Kings Saul and Solomon, they believe their own hype and grandeur. Over time, they become so beholden to their need for power they've achieved via their branded platform that they fail to notice when the spirit shifts. Over time, their empires crumble under the weight of irrelevance.[5]

Roger, however, kept true to the core of who he was and continued to embody the quality of justice outlined by Comte-Sponville that to "be just in the moral sense, is to refuse to place oneself above the law or above one's fellowman."[6] Once Roger secured the original charter for Rhode Island on March 14, 1644, he could have returned and ruled the roost. Finally, after years of poverty and hardship, he had the ability to secure enough property and funds to build a house large enough to contain his wife and eventual six children, not to mention a drawing room where he could entertain guests and other accoutrements afforded fine gentlemen of his newfound social standing.

Instead, Roger refused to grant himself the usual privileges of leadership. He put himself on the same level of his fellow citizens

---

find individuals who justify their decisions on the basis of a word from God or the stirring of Jesus in their heart. (More often than not, these rumblings would probably be diagnosed as some form of faith based flatulence—think less God and more gas.) These books focusing on the topic of narcissism, psychopathy, and sociopathy offer good primers for those wishing to explore this topic in greater depth: Burgo, *The Narcissist You Know;* Hare, *Without Conscience;* James,*The Narcissist Next Door;* MacKenzie, *Psychopath Free;* Malkin, *Rethinking Narcissism;* and Stout, *The Sociopath Next Door.*

This survey may be small in scope but its findings regarding the preponderance of narcissism in even seeming liberal Canadian clergy are eye opening. See Puls and Gall, "Frequency of Narcissistic Personality Disorder."

5. See 1 Samuel and 1&2 Kings/1&2 Chronicles respectively. This dynamic is especially true for those Christian voices who proclaim to be prophets and social justice pioneers but yet continue to operate in an outdated white male missional model. Their conversations about "doing church" fail to address the radical shifts taking place in more liberal churches and spiritual but not religious circles in creating spaces that fully embrace women, people of color, and LGBTQ+ folks as integral members and leaders of a given faith community. For examples of the theological changes transpiring in liberal Christendom, check out Cheng, *Rainbow Theology.*

6. *A Small Treatise*, 73.

by refusing to take the bulk of the land for himself but continued to broker fair treaties with the local tribes to obtain additional land as needed to accommodate the growing colony.

Throughout his life as a leader of the colony, he displayed a number of similar actions that demonstrated his belief that all Rhode Islanders were to be treated as equals. For example, he adopted the same position later advocated by US President George Washington by agreeing to serve only for a limited time period. Both leaders expressed similar concerns that one person should not hold too much power for an extended period of time. Roger last played a public role during King Phillip's War (1675–76). Despite his actions to keep the Narragansetts out of the war, his house was burned to the ground during the attack and he was plunged into poverty.[7]

Even on his deathbed, Roger continued to put the needs of others ahead of his own. In his final days, to quote his son Daniel, "He gave away his lands and other estate, to them that he thought were most in want, until he gave away all."[8]

Native Justice

We see Roger's selfless striving for justice most clearly in his interactions with Indigenous people. Here, he delineated between laws which secured rights to all residents of Rhode Island and laws which discriminated against groups or individuals disliked by the majority or those in power. Comte-Sponville defines this distinction. "Just or not, the law is still the law; no democracy, no republic would be possible if people obeyed only those laws they approved of. True, but no democracy or republic would be acceptable if obedience required us to abjure justice or tolerate the intolerable."[9]

When he first arrived in this territory, some historians suggest he paid a visit to Massasoit (Ousamequin), the sachem of

---

7 For more in-depth coverage of this event, see *Creation of the American Soul*, 385–387.

8. *Memoir of Roger Williams*, 111.

9. *A Small Treatise*, 65.

Pokanoket who resided at Mt. Hope.[10] From Massasoit, he secured a grant for a patch of land that included the town of Seekonk in Massachusetts. Since this town was within the limits of Plymouth Colony, Roger could have just taken Seekonk and claimed it for his own. Instead, he perceived correctly that Indigenous people were the only rightful proprietors of all property situated in what eventually became known as the United States of America. Unfortunately, he had to give up this land after the leaders in the Massachusetts Bay Colony brought the hammer down on the smaller Plymouth Colony and Roger was forced to move eastward. There he negotiated with the Narragansett sachems Cononicus and Miantonomo for the land that formed the city of Providence.

The agreements to buy the property that eventually became the state of Rhode Island appear to follow the same principles Roger employed when obtaining his first bit of property from Massasoit.[11] Some historians observed how in their estimation, he never exploited and pillaged Indigenous people's land in the name of a particular country or commercial entity as the vast majority of those founding the other colonies did with increasing regularity.

His early primer on the languages of the local tribes, *A Key to the Language of America, or a help to the Languages of the Natives in that part of America Called New-England* (1643), is the first printed vocabulary of this kind. In lieu of dismissing Indigenous people as pagan savages spiritually inferior to the European settlers, Roger took the time to learn about their tribal practices and religious beliefs.[12] Also, Roger labored with them on their land where he grew food that he and his family used to survive.

In addition, Roger started a trading post at Cocumscussoc (now North Kingstown) where he traded with the local tribes. He sold this trading post in 1651 to finance his return trip to England. The very principles that got him expelled from the

10. Mt. Hope is situated near present day Bristol, RI.

11. For details regarding this transactions see Carter Roger Williams Initiative, "Original Land Deed to Providence."

12. For more information about this work, see Carter Roger Williams Initiative, "A Key into the Language of America."

Massachusetts Bay Colony formed the basis of creating a just society in Rhode Island. In his ongoing interactions with both the local tribes and those settlers who called Rhode Island home, he sought to do what he felt was right rather than do what would be deemed profitable and popular.

One could argue that in these interactions Roger pioneered the concept of international justice in North America if not the world. He became the first person in the Western civilized world to push the notion of a state built on liberty of conscience where citizens move beyond simply tolerating the other, into a vision of justice for all. He showed a way to "be" with the other rather than putting himself front and center, even though this way of being entailed some significant personal sacrifices including giving up his home in Salem, loss of social standing, and any hope of a fortune.[13]

> 13. In his work with the Narragansetts and other local tribes, we see signs of Roger defying the evangelical missionary mindset that one finds present today in even allegedly progressive settings by treating all as equals. This formula seems to apply whether one is sent out to the missionary fields to minister to the "other" albeit brown or black babies situated below the Equator or LGBTQ+ teens thrown out of their homes by their fundamentalist parents.
>
>   1. A believer (or maybe a fallen soul who backslid) has a moment of clarity when they realize they must do something to reach out to the other so their faith can become alive again.
>   2. So they go into the wilds of the jungle or gayborhoods of the United States and begin to blog about their experiences. A bit of research often reveals that for most of these folks their "research" consists of chatting with their one buddy from Wheaton College who just came out of the closet or their selective missionary experiences where they were escorted around by staffers from some evangelical outreach organization. The bulk of their remaining research consists of quoting their fellow progressive author/speaker/pastors, the majority of whom are cisgender, white, and male. In a few rare instances, a gay, African American, or even a female author can be permitted to speak once they have been vetted to ensure they will stick to the well established script. And so the theological circle jerk continues round and round and round with the sounds from this echo chamber drowning out any dissenting voices.
>   3. These experiences transformed them into new kinds of Christians where another world is possible. At this point, if these pseudo-progressives built up enough interest among other like minded souls, they

JUSTICE

Rhode Island once again made social justice history when on May 18, 1652, the colony passed the first ban on lifetime and gender slavery. When the Founding Fathers sat down to craft the Declaration of Independence and the original Constitution over a hundred years later, they could not follow Roger's example.[14]

---

      begin to explore publishing options that will enable them to talk about their journey out of the Christian closet towards a more tolerant theology. The stories of those they encounter are helpful to the extent these tales allow them to craft their narrative of forgiveness for having once been so narrow minded re the other until they now see the light and realize that poor and gay people are lovable and kind (you know like puppies). Trans folks tend to be icky so they don't go there.

4. Should #3 prove to be successful, these newly minted apologists get invited to churches and other faith groups where they talk about their experiences with the natives. This serves three purposes: a) builds a platform for the newly discovered author/speaker; b) allows those in attendance to feel as though surely they can't be homophobic/misogynist/racist/classist, etc. because after all, they came to hear this author/speaker who is being denounced by hard line reformers like John Piper and Mark Driscoll for their allegedly groundbreaking work; and c) sparks the interest of another potential author/speaker missionary so the cycle can continue. (And in the case of LGBTQ+ issues, the speaker also hopes to attracts a few closeted fundies who will then begin to e-mail the author as they feel someone finally "gets them." These souls provide fodder for additional research and prove their street cred as being pro-gay for having connected with the "homosexual" heart.)

5. They will not support whatever political/ecclesiological issues are fundamental to these natives out of concern that they need to keep dialoguing with those who have yet to see the light. These in the dark as it were tend to be their biggest funders so one questions if appeasement or illumination is the driving force here.

6. This dynamic spread in recent years to those mainline bodies looking for new ways of doing church. They fail to realize that "church" has become a dying institution and that for their faith to grow, they must exit á la Roger and see what's beyond the institutional horizons. I've penned enough books on this topic to know now is the time to 'fold 'em and walk away,' to paraphrase Kenny Rogers's "The Gambler."

14. Slavery officially ended in the US in 1865, see "13th Amendment to the U.S. Constitution: Abolition of Slavery." However, this battle remains far from over. In the 21st century, slavery affects more than 40 million people worldwide. See Nodal, "Slavery Affects More than 40 Million."

15

Civil Rights for All

Roger demonstrated his support of rights for women during an era when women were still viewed as property of their husbands who had no voice in any public capacity whatsoever.[16] His astoundingly progressive view of women was evidenced in the first recorded conflict in Rhode Island, which arose over the application of the law of liberty when Jane Verin, the wife of Joshua Verin, desired to

---

15. Hayward, "Smart Women are Evil."

16. Women secured the right to vote throughout the US when Amendment 19 of the US Constitution was ratified on August 18, 1920. See "19th Amendment to the U.S. Constitution: Women's Right to Vote."

avail herself of Roger's ministry.[17] The Verins came to Providence in the Spring of 1636 where they obtained a lot next to the Williams's home. While Joshua chose not to attend the religious meetings held in Roger's home, his wife Jane began coming to these meetings against her husband's wishes. In retaliation, Joshua beat her until "she went in danger of life."

The town met to reprimand Joshua both for his physical abuse, as well as violating his wife's liberty of conscience. At the town meeting, an act was passed where "It was agreed that Joshua Verin, upon breach of covenant for restraining liberty of conscience, shall be withheld from liberty of voting until he shall declare the contrary."[18] Now, Joshua was never formally prosecuted for his abuse, nor did the colony intervene on Jane's behalf when he moved with her to Salem. Still, Roger must be considered a forward thinker on women's rights when one compares the Verin case with the Puritan view of the "weaker"–and untrustworthy–sex that continues to inform today's political debates around legislating women's bodies.

Contemporary issues pertaining to human sexuality such as abortion, contraception, and sexual harassment were discussed in different words in the 1600s. Also, Roger would not perform marriages because like other Puritan clergy of his time and place, he viewed the formalizing of this union as purely a civil matter.[19] Hence, as I noted earlier, we cannot apply Roger's teachings directly to all topics that dominate the US political landscape in the twenty-first century. Assessing Roger's stance that justice is the inherent right of every individual, one could conclude that regardless of his personal convictions, he would side with those who wish to exercise their religious beliefs as long as they remain separated from the state.[20] I base this assumption on analyzing his interac-

---

17. National Park Service, "Roger Williams: The Verin Case."

18. *Life of Roger Williams*, 51.

19. For a brief history of marriage, see Joyce, "Coupling and Culture."

20. As noted previously, Roger remained a strict Calvinist to the core. So one can safely assume that in his personal life, he represented the epitome of a morally upright citizen and kept his pants on. Given he had six children, he

tions with the Quakers. Roger possessed that rare ability to set aside his personal prejudice against the Quakers and allowed them to reside within the colony he founded.[21] In fact, he even assisted Anne Hutchinson and crew in purchasing what is now the town of Portsmouth from the Narragansett tribe.

This acceptance of outcasts got put to the test from 1658 to 1661 when severe laws were passed in the Massachusetts Bay Colony against the Quakers. They became subjected to capital or corporal punishment that in the cases of Mary Dyer and a few others resulted in death.[22] Despite intense pressure from these leaders to join in this crackdown, Roger refused to persecute those Quakers who resided within the confines of Rhode Island. Even when King Charles II issued an order in September 1661 that all Quakers residing in the colonies be sent back to England where they would be subjected to capital or corporal punishment, there's no evidence Rhode Island obeyed said order.

As he allowed the Quakers to come in and quake as they pleased, extended religious liberty to women who were viewed as their husband's property, and treated Indigenous people as the rightful owners of their land, and thus deserving of fair and appropriate compensation for their property, I feel confident the founder of the first Baptist church in America would also extend justice to LGBTQ+ folks currently being ostracized by twenty-first century Southern Baptists who refuse to allow them to receive the same rights granted to other US citizens.[23] For under Roger's rule, all were welcome into this itty-bitty spot of land that anyone could call home.[24]

---

clearly took them off on more than one occasion.

21. The history books do not recount any incidents of the Quakers pulling moves in Rhode Island like getting butt nekkid in public as they were wont to do in Massachusetts They seen to settle down a bit once they were in a colony that left them alone.

22. For a more in-depth account of Dyer's death, see Christianity.com, "Mary Dyer Hanged for 'Wrong' Faith."

23. For the latest news from the Southern Baptist Convention (SBC) regarding same sex marriages, see their "On 'Same-Sex Marriage."

24. Doubtful though that Rhode Island would ever become an LGBTQ+

playland a la Provincetown, Fire Island, or the Castro. Call it a hunch.

25. Hayward, "Heavenly Homosexuals."

5
Courage

GIVEN ROGER CAME OF age during a turbulent time in England's religious and political history, one cannot presume if his father's pleas that Roger remain part of the Anglican fold were more out of concern for his soul or his safety. But as noted earlier, from the age of 11 onwards, Roger was his own man.

By the time he was a student at Pembroke College, he undoubtedly heard about Alexander Leighton's plight after the publication of his pamphlet "Zion's Plea Against Prelacy: An Appeal to Parliament" in 1628. Under Charles I, Leighton was committed to prison for life, fined 10,000 pounds, and degraded from his ministry. Then he was whipped and pilloried with his ears cut off, his nose slit, and his face branded with a hot iron.[1] All that's missing is talk about doing something to his bottom and bits, and you've got the makings of a classic Monty Python skit.

Comte-Sponville informs us that "all the virtues are interdependent and they all depend on courage."[2] Without this virtue, men become armchair activists sniffing brandy as they talk about the need to stand up for social justice, their desire to be prudent, and so forth and so on. These men tend to be known more for their hemorrhoids than their heroics. Plato's definition of courage centers on knowing what is right and acting only on that

---

1. This story is recounted in "A Biographical Introduction," *The Bloudy Tenent*.
2. *A Small Treatise*, 59.

knowledge.[3] To most people's minds, courage is morally neutral. Comte-Sponville quotes Voltaire as a reminder that to most people, "courage is not a virtue [in and of itself] but a quality shared by blackguards and great men alike."[4] Those who are virtuously courageous can endure risk without selfish motivation–though they pursue their quests in moderation. Before committing an act, the courageous prudently ask themselves if the risks they might incur justify the desired end result. For instance, risking one's life to save a child who fell into a well would be a courageous act. But diving down head first into the same well thus killing both self and child would qualify one more for a Darwin Award than a Red Badge of Courage.[5]

After Roger became a chaplain to Sir Masham and was already friends with Coke, he could have played his cards right and been well on his way to a comfy lifestyle and a prominent place within the annals of history. Unlike those quasi-affirming souls who can appease both crown and conscience, Roger never could toe the party line. Given the lack of correspondence pertaining to his courtship of Jane Whalley, we cannot ascertain if he chose to break social protocol deliberately by courting out of his league or if he possessed a naive spirit that truly believed a Horatio Alger type story could be possible within the social stratification of seventeenth century England. Once he got the unceremonious boot from the Masham estate, he did not appear to ruminate over the loss of his comfortable position. Rather, he accepted his newfound fate and moved on.

Historians speculate he got his courage from Coke, whom Roger appeared to view more as a father figure than his own father. Throughout his life, he always spoke lovingly of Coke while seldom mentioning his father except in passing. During his time as Coke's scribe, he saw how deftly Coke managed to battle the crown and come out ahead with his principles intact. But having witnessed

3. See Plato, *Republic,* 429a-430c for a fuller description of Plato's thoughts on courage.

4. *A Small Treatise,* 45.

5. See Crane, *The Red Badge of Courage* and "The Darwin Awards."

King James I send Coke to the Tower for contradicting the King to his face, Roger also knew the cost that he might incur when he came of age and began to voice his own anti-Royalist sentiments.

He took the strands of religious liberty woven by Coke and his other contemporaries and crafted them into a flag he began waving all around, proclaiming religious liberty for all. We have no accurate depictions of Roger in action, but I like to imagine him as a swaggering young Han Solo from *Star Wars* barreling ahead to rescue us all from the sin of commingling the church with the state. This image remains but a fantasy since I cannot think of a single Williams relative I have ever met who actually fits this description of a handsome rebel warrior.[6]

Roger's letters convey a man certain in his convictions with the will to live them in every moment of his life, both personal and public. I can barely comprehend the kind of courage running through his veins that gave him the strength to be the first person in the Western Hemisphere to demand that "religious liberty" be written into the law books. Other Puritan divines danced around the notion of keeping the crown out of the church's business, but he was the first actually to stand up and demand that these two conjoined entities become separated. More importantly, he actually put these principles into practice.

By the time Roger arrived in Boston, his ideas about religious liberty had crystallized to the point where he began to preach with increased fervor. Even his fellow Puritans asked him to temper his rhetoric when he began to proclaim the need for "soul liberty," a term that means neither the state nor the church can judge the conscience of even the heretic or atheist. I find it next to impossible to imagine the Christian cojones it took for anyone to stand before the Puritan mob and later the Anglican inbred Parliament and acknowledge that atheists have the right not to believe in God.

---

6. For an interesting take on Roger's rebel heritage see Barry, "Roger Williams, America's First Rebel."

7

After Roger got kicked out of Boston, the folks in Salem embraced him. This was approximately fifty years before the infamous Salem Witch trials. So the town hadn't lost its sanity—yet.[8] At this juncture in history, these folks seemed to be closer to his beliefs in terms of worshiping according to scripture and their desire to be free from the crown regarding their religious practices. As Salem was perceived to be a backwater town when compared to Boston, the more refined Bostonians tended to leave these hicks alone. But within a relatively short time, Roger's radical ways began to cause divisions in Salem as well, and he set off for Plymouth.

7. Photo taken during Pope Benedict's visit to New York City in April 2008. See Garrison, "The Pope vs. Spiderman."

8. For a short summary of this era in history, see Blumberg, "A Brief History of the Salem Witch Trials."

Since Roger arrived in Plymouth Colony about eleven years after the Pilgrims arrived on the Mayflower, I presume he connected with my Pilgrim ancestors John Howland, Elizabeth Tilley, John Alden, and Priscilla Mullins. According to the record books, they would still be living in the area, and Plymouth Colony was small enough that I suspect he became acquainted with the vast majority of the colonists.[9] Except for Bradford, Roger seldom mentioned any of the residents by name.

Roger corresponded at length about his conversations with Indigenous people, and alienated the leaders in Boston, Salem, and Plymouth when he argued that the royal charter did not allow them to take land away from Indigenous people without reasonable compensation. Treating the local tribes with the dignity and respect afforded male property holders of the ruling class proved to be an unthinkable concept for just about anyone else.[10]

In his later correspondence, he reflected fondly on his time in Plymouth. Those who came over on the Mayflower seemed to manifest a more liberal spirit than what he experienced especially in Boston. These Pilgrims came from Holland and as such, they were entirely alienated from the Church of England. I presume they found Roger's requests to disengage from the crown less jarring than did those in the Massachusetts Bay Colony, who wished to remain on good terms with the crown for the purposes of

---

9. See State Library of Massachusetts, "Mayflower Passengers," for the exact years that each of my Mayflower relatives died. During a press trip to Plymouth and the surrounding environs, I was intrigued by the Howland and Alden homes once inhabited by my ancestors. I cried a bit inside when I came to the common grave marking the spot where about half the Pilgrims who died the first winter in the New World were buried. Included in the mix were Elizabeth Tilly's and Priscilla Mullins's parents. Orphaned as teens in a new world, no wonder they married the much older John Howland and John Alden respectively. Despite Longfellow's 1858 poem "The Courtship of Miles Standish" that depicts a romanticized view of John's courtship of Priscilla, these marriages struck me as more born out of necessity than love. While these two marriages lasted for decades until death with no reports of spousal abuse, I do wonder how many Colonial era women had their own #metoo experiences. But again, I digress.

10. For more background into how Winthrop's profits conflicted with William's prophecy, see Lehman, *The Money Cult*.

preserving their charter and vested financial interests. Framing these debates in purely religious terms ignores the commercial motivations for establishing new territories. I chose not to stress this point since Roger appeared to be about as disinterested in finances as I am, but we cannot totally ignore the cha-ching that has driven US Christianity from the moment Europeans colonized the Americas from the native populations already living there.

Like Roger, the Pilgrims wished to worship free from interference by the crown. Unlike Roger, they insisted on religious conformity within their colony. One could not live in Plymouth unless one was willing to join their community and worship at their church. Over time, the honeymoon ended over Roger's insistent preaching against this requirement that everyone must share the same religious beliefs. So Roger journeyed back to Salem to assist his friend, the ailing Rev. Samuel Skelton, a move that raised the hackles of the Massachusetts Bay Colony.

Faced with the choice of passage to England, and likely at the very least a nasty slitting of the nose, or heading out into the wild, Roger chose the latter. Initially, the leaders of Massachusetts declared he could stay in Salem until spring as long as he refrained from preaching. Roger agreed to cease any public pronouncements, but continued to hold private meetings in his home. Those in power did not take too kindly to Roger violating the spirit of their law. Before a crowd could gather together and venture up to Salem and forcibly remove Roger from his abode, his good friend Winthrop tipped him off that he should flee his home lickety-split.

So Roger headed out in the dead of a New England winter. He recounts his struggle to leave behind his wife and two daughters, being prudent enough to realize they could not survive this harsh winter. John Cotton claims some people went ahead and made provisions of housing and other necessities. Gaustad refutes this assertion, citing that after his expulsion from the Massachusetts Bay Colony, Roger "would wander for 14 weeks in bitter snow and a 'howling wilderness' not knowing what 'bed or bread did mean.'"[11]

11. Gaustad, *Roger Williams*, 14. In his quest for the truth, Socrates was

While he had begun to converse with the local tribes during his time in Plymouth, Roger had conducted those conversations in an environment where at least he had food and shelter. In this vulnerable state where he needed their assistance to provide him with the basic necessities to keep him alive, he had no clue if they would actually welcome him in. Fortunately the local tribes extended the hand of kindness; Roger survived the winter, and his relationship with them continued to deepen.

During the Pequot Wars of 1637–38, Roger's negotiating skills were called into service.[12] He knew from his interactions and friendships with the Narragansett tribe that they would protect him and his family, even though the warrior Pequot tribe was out for blood and had killed John Oldham, another known friend of the Narragansett tribe. While his own life might not be on the line, if Roger failed to dissuade the local tribes from coalescing into a powerful league, then other colonists' lives would be in jeopardy. He forged ahead, and after three days of intense negotiations, the local tribes did not form a league, which would have certainly resulted in a bloody war.

He kept negotiating with the local tribes even during the 1670s when a series of hostile incidents between Plymouth Colony and the Wampanoag sachem King Philip (Metacom) led to the devastating conflict known as King Philip's War, which involved the Narragansett tribe and extended to all of Massachusetts, Connecticut, and Rhode Island.[13] Despite Roger's negotiations with local tribal elders, some of their younger members set the town of Providence on fire. But as a sign of respect, they guided Roger out of the conflict, thus preventing the Williams family from going up in flames as well.

---

forced to drink hemlock and died a painful death from poisoning. When put into this context, I suppose banishment in the dead of winter seems a little bit better.

12. Information about these battles can be found by logging on to Mashantucket Pequot Museum, "Battlefields of the Pequot War."

13. For additional details about this forgotten bit of US History, go to National Park Service, "Roger Williams: King Philip's War."

Shortly after this war, his wife Mary died. Roger soldiered on to rebuild both the colony and his relationship with the local tribes. Rhode Island rose from the ashes, though the friendships with the local tribes that Roger nurtured disintegrated soon after his death. None of his successors possessed the courage of Roger's convictions to practice a form of radical inclusion that truly welcomed all.

> It is when we stop believing that religions have been handed down from above or else that they are entirely daft that matters become more interesting. We can then recognize that we invented religions to serve two central needs which continue to this day and which secular society has not been able to solve with any particular skill: first, the need to live together in communities in harmony, despite our deeply rooted selfish and violent impulses. And secondly, the need to cope with terrifying degrees of pain which arise from our vulnerability to professional failure, to troubled relationships, to the death of loved ones and to our decay and demise.
>
> —ALAIN DE BOTTON, *Religion for Atheists*[14]

---

14. de Botton, *Religion for Atheists*, 12.

6
Temperance

COULD A MAN WITH enough backbone to stand up to the British crown during a time of mass persecution of Puritans more moderate than himself possess any signs he could temper his spirit? According to Comte-Sponville's definition of temperance, the answer would be "yes." He defines temperance as "the moderation which allows us to be masters of our pleasure instead of becoming its slaves."[1] Then he discusses how this virtue gets lived out in practice. "Temperance is prudence applied to pleasure, the point being to enjoy as much as possible as well as is possible, by intensifying sensation of our consciousness of it and not by multiplying the objects of pleasure ad infinitum."[2]

In Roger's case, his ardor and passion led some to view him as obstinate. But this was balanced by his being upright and pious, with a very giving and forgiving nature.[3] One of his biographers described him as "one of the most disinterested men that ever lived; a most pious and heavenly-minded soul."[4]

While his enemies found fault with his ideas, they never slammed his moral character. For example, John Cotton's grandson Cotton Mather, who wrote in an elaborate insult that Roger had "a

---

1. *A Small Treatise*, 39.
2. *A Small Treatise*, 40.
3. For a further examination of Roger's personal piety, his book *Experiments of Spiritual Health* reveals his prayer life and reliance on the grace of God.
4. *Memoir of Roger Williams*, 388.

windmill in his head," also admitted that Roger generally had, as another biographer put it, *"the root of the matter* in his heart."[5]

Another man might have utilized these sentiments of goodwill to craft a state modeled on his interpretation of justice that would be carried out by like-minded souls. Instead, Roger encouraged the cacophony in the public square as a living embodiment of his belief that genuine freedom can only be fully actualized when all are free to express their views. Roger prevented his colony, and arguably much of the world, from authoritarianism, from letting justice become misunderstood as abject loyalty.

When handling ongoing disputes among both Indigenous people and his fellow Rhode Islanders, Roger displayed wonderful tact and sagacity. In a similar vein, his debates with his friend Winthrop retained that "gentlemanly cordiality" all too lacking among contemporary bombastic bible thumpers. Roger's and Winthrop's ability to engage in intelligent dialogue and discourse over theological and political issues, while maintaining a civil tone as they agreed to disagree, should be the gold standard that all, myself included, should strive to achieve.

Along those lines, whenever he was asked by Winthrop to resolve conflicts with Indigenous people, Roger would graciously step forward even though he remained banished from the Massachusetts Bay Colony. Simply put, spitefulness and revenge were not part of his DNA. Roger returned good for evil at every turn.

Roger's correspondence with Mrs. Anne Sadlier, the daughter of Coke, shows his ability to remain graceful and humble when greeted with insolence. During his second trip to London circa 1663, he felt a longing to connect to the legacy of his mentor who had died two years after Roger went to America. So he penned a letter to Coke's surviving daughter apologizing for his absence and praising her late father. In her curt reply, she dismissed his work with acerbic phrases like "new lights that are so much cried up will prove but dark lanterns."[6] She demonstrated her full disdain for his critiques of the late King Charles I, stating "none but a villain such

---

5. *Makers of American History*, 161.
6. *Roger Williams: A Study*, 203–204.

as yourself would have wrote them."[7] Somehow, Roger managed to maintain his decorum and not answer in kind.

A few historians speculate that her lack of courtesy towards Roger indicates that the relationship between Roger and Coke was exaggerated, but this analysis doesn't explain Roger's flowing praise of their relationship over the years. Roger was as honest and truthful as they come. His character would not permit him to pretend he had a close relationship with someone of Coke's stature if this were not in fact the case.

Some history books depict Roger as a lone wolf. Though he clearly remained his own man, we can see starting with Coke how others informed his character. His virtuous qualities didn't arise in a vacuum, but were molded by relationships with Coke and others. Even when he was alone in the dead of winter, those Indigenous people who found him were already his friends. Roger's life is a shining example of the need for each of us to remain connected to some type of community that can nurture us. During his lifetime Rhode Island remained a welcoming community for all comers instead of becoming an exclusionary WASP enclave where only the elect could enter.

---

7. *Roger Williams: A Study*, 204.

TEMPERANCE

8

8. Series of shotgun shells I placed in the form of a cross to symbolize the church militant.

7
Roger and Me: My Journey from Christian to Spiritual Seeker

WHEN I BEGAN MY research into Roger around 2009, I still considered myself a professional "Christian" author.[1] But like Roger, I found myself walking away from the institutional church. And similarly to some of Roger's words in *The Bloudy Tenent*, I used my book *Jesus Died for This?* as a satirical sword to slay those who still remained connected to the Christian Industrial Complex. Subtle is not a word I'd use to describe either of our attacks on those who try to force their brand of Christianity into civil law.

During my travels from 2010 through 2012 to promote this book, I found myself slowly shifting from "Christian" satirist/author to spiritual storyteller/satirist. While sitting in on a session at the 2012 South by Southwest (SXSW) festival titled "Bridging the Digital and the Divine,"[2] I became acutely aware of the silliness in trying to devise spiritual content optimized to generate online traffic. Lost in this conversation was the rise of atheist clergy and

---

1. Even though we're related, I never read any of Roger's works until my middle years. At Yale Divinity School (1988–1992) I studied the history of liberal Protestantism. In this context, Roger was referenced, but we did not peruse the original sources. When I finally delved into his works, I was stunned at the similarity of our thinking. While deciphering seventeenth century English can be quite a challenge, I could see how portions of his work almost directly paralleled pieces I had penned. Given I had not read his work until after my book *Red and Blue God, Black and Blue Church* was published, I concluded that somehow Roger's essence must be imbedded in my genetic code.

2. See SXSW, "Bridging the Digital and the Divine."

secular spiritual communities, as well as outlier religious gatherings, a development I tuned into back in 2007.[3]

But I caught a glimpse of this secular spiritual spirit when I caught Kelly Carlin's *A Carlin Home Companion* at the same SXSW Festival.[4] Here I became privy to an intimate glimpse into the soul of a man who saved me. My Episcopal priest/sociology professor father introduced me to *Laugh In, The Smothers Brothers Comedy Hour,* Tom Lehrer, and other inappropriate fare for small children. How many nine-year-olds can recite both "The Lord's Prayer"[5] and "The Vatican Rag" while giving Tricky Dick the finger (with full parental approval I might add)? So naturally I connected with her late father George Carlin and savored his move from a beloved sixties hippy dippy weatherman character to counter-cultural icon.[6]

Carlin's critiques of Americana culture—and religion in particular—helped keep me sane when my family's sixties era idealism morphed into alcoholism during the "me generation" that defined the seventies. My father died all alone the day I turned 16, which explains my visceral disgust for the Sweet Sixteen song stylings of Neil Sedaka.[7] Eleven months later, I became orphaned, with scant familial support that has only lessened with time. Without Carlin's biting critiques coupled with the absurdity of Monty Python's Flying Circus, I feel confident I would be pushing

---

3. See Garrison, "Atheist Pastor Deemed Unsuitable for Ministry" as one example of a an atheist clergy person and The Clergy Project, which points to a larger trend of clergy declaring themselves as atheists. In addition, Cox and Jones's comprehensive 2017 survey "America's Changing Religious Identity" documents this shift towards the growth of people who are religiously unaffiliated yet do not consider themselves to be atheists per se. Also, in my book *The New Atheists Crusaders*, 166–167, I report on my first encounter with Greg Epstein, Humanist chaplain at Harvard University. Through his connections, I began reporting on the rise of atheist clergy and secular spiritual communities.

4. See Carlin, *A Carlin Home Companion.*

5. Matt 6:9–13 and Luke 11:2–4.

6. See Zoglin, "How George Carlin Changed Comedy."

7. See Sedaka, "Happy Birthday Sweet Sixteen."

daisies (though with my extended family's history, I'd probably end up as fertilizer for kudzu).[8]

When Kelly walked us through her parents' deaths, I could almost feel her touching what the Celts term "thin space"—that line that separates this world from the next. (Not to turn into *Lion King* mush here—anything Disneyfied tends to turn my stomach.[9]) By the end of her piece, I saw more than Carlin's smile in Kelly. I could feel his genetic code embedded in her DNA, which she reinterpreted through her own unique life lens. Her father is embedded in her bones just as Roger is in me.[10]

Later, while attending a screening of *Let Fury Have the Hour* at the 2012 Tribeca Film Festival, comedian Lewis Black's rants reminded me there is no inside- or outside-the-box thinking.[11] Instead, there's just thinking. Boxless is beautiful. Time for me to just throw all my Christian cardboard into the trash can.

Seems I'm not alone in trashing my childhood thinking about God. Some self-proclaimed church experts continue to preach, "If you build a better church, they will come." The actual statistics tell another story. According to a 2017 survey of Americans' religious practices, this landscape is undergoing a dramatic transformation. "White Christians, once the dominant religious group in the U.S., now account for fewer than half of all adults living in the country. Today, fewer than half of all states are majority white Christian."[12] With the ongoing exodus of people leaving institutionalized Christianity, could we see the demise of Americana branded Christianity?

By the time I moved from the Northeast to Portland, Oregon in 2014, I no longer marketed myself to the "Christian" market. I

---

8. I go more in to detail regarding my parents' deaths in Garrison, *Jesus Died for This?*, 121–130.

9. *The Lion King.*

10. An earlier version of these reflections can be found in my article "Coming Home to a Carlin Companion."

11. *Let Fury Have the Hour.*

12. See Cox and Jones, "America's Changing Religious Identity."

began exploring the sacred sexuality and spirituality of the Celtic ethos inspired by the natural beauty of the Pacific Northwest.[13]

I still dip my feet in the rituals of the Anglican Church because the Eucharist remains how this former altar girl remembers her daddy. He baptized her at six weeks old, prepped her for confirmation when she was eleven, and taught her how to serve alongside him at the altar a year later. When asked about my faith journey, I say I'm an apophatic agnostic Anglican.[14] I don't have all

---

13. After moving to Portland, among those ministers, pastors, and priests I found reaching out to those for whom church is not in their vocabulary included Angie & Todd Fadel, Ken & Deborah Loyd, Kurt Neilson, and Karen Ward. For more information about the Fadels's and Loyds's work see Escobar, *Down We Go*. Neilson's and Ward's ministries are referenced in Garrison, *Ancient Future Disciples*.

Also, my piece in *The Humanist* points to the emergence of alternative communities in PDX. See Garrison, "Lots of Love."

14. In my November 2011 interview with Eileen Flynn, I observed that I consider myself to be an apophatic Anglican. Since this interview, I now add agnostic into the mix. See Flynn, "Q&A: Author Becky Garrison."

As I've noted somewhat in jest, my responses to my childhood appeared to be cyanide or satire. Given my resilient nature, I chose the latter. This story points to one of the odd ways my childhood faith shaped me into a satirist.

In 1972–73, the Garrison clan attended bi-weekly services at the Roosevelt Warms Springs Institute for Rehabilitation located in Warm Springs, Georgia. My father served on the rota of their supply clergy who would perform on Sundays and church holidays. Whenever I worked as dad's altar girl, he would often break wind while I was helping him prepare the elements for communion. After doing his business, he would give a look in my direction so the entire congregation thought I was responsible for the anti-incense odor wafting through the diminutive chapel.

But during the Christmas Eve service, dad managed to rise above this stench. Right before communion, a few orderlies wheeled in those patients, who were bedridden. My eyes connected briefly with a boy who couldn't have been more than a few years older than me. In another context, we might have become friends, perhaps even dated. But based on his gaunt appearance, I would be surprised if he made it much beyond New Year's Day. When I saw him smile as he took communion from my father, I could see for a brief moment how my dad could still truly touched those in need instead of simply caressing his own bloated drunken ego. In this nanosecond, I saw the fiery soul of a 25-year old priest trying to integrate his small town Southern parish circa 1959. Before he tuned out with Timothy Leary, this sociology professor researched how to connect with outcasts raging from the Students for a

the answers, but I will continue to ask questions while embracing the mysteries of life. For now, I choose to keep "Anglican" in my identity as a vestige from my childhood. I still connect to rituals from my Episcopal days like walking a labyrinth or—very infrequently—partaking of the Eucharist, even though these acts no longer carry any Jesus-y sensations for me.

I found my soul through offerings like The Round, a monthly gathering consisting of three musicians and a slam poet, who gather in places ranging from a church basement to bars and parks.[15] They perform rounds of poetry and music while a visual artist creates a painting that depicts their own perceptions of this collective energy. The fusion of these art forms connects artists and audience in unison that feels more connected and spiritual than what I've experienced in a traditional church service. The Rev. Karen Ward, Pastor of Rose City Park UMC and Church of the Beloved and Director of Portland Abbey Arts, observes, "The whole point is there is no split. Renewed human community is sacred no matter if there's a religious overlay or not."[16]

Similarly, ecstatic dance and other practices with a tantric energy allow me to explore sacred sexuality through movement and music in secular yet spiritual settings.[17]

My return to the Pacific Northwest enabled me to resume my work with Gary Austin, founder of the Groundlings during

---

Democratic Society (SDS) to the Jesus People USA. Could this night be a sobering experience in more ways than one?

However, the next time we visited Warm Springs Chapel, dad was back to SNAFU spirituality, encouraging us to reenact the miracle of the loaves and fishes by overindulging courtesy of the free buffet tickets given to the visiting minister and his family. (See Matt. 14:13–21, Mark 6:31–44, Luke 9:10–17 and John 6:5–15.)

"God bless. The food's free. Chow down, kids."

Another distorted lesson in God's grace delivered by my Monty Python-esque priestly father. So much for divine intervention. A much shorter version of this story can be found at Garrison, *The New Atheist Crusaders*, 153–154.

15. See Portland Abbey Arts.
16. Ward, E-mail.
17. See Roth, "5Rhythms" and Garrison, "Embracing the Six Types Of Love." For an introduction to tantric practices, see "Art of Being."

his occasional teaching treks to Seattle.[18] When I first connected with Gary in 1996, I was based in New York City and looking for a teacher who could help me physicalize my words by getting me out of my head and into my body. Gary taught me that when my top priority is for my work to make sense, I will end up with boring, predictable "sense." But when I take a risk and follow my intuition—even if it feels like nonsense—the audience will make connections to my words that I didn't know existed.

Under Gary's guidance, my work evolved from jokey, top-ten lists to satire that exposes the underbelly of the institutional church that caused both of us, and so many others, to walk away. The more truth I uncovered, the less I knew. And the less I believed.

After he died on April Fools Day 2017, I felt like a piece of me crumbled as well. I don't have delusions of keeping Gary beside me like a cardboard character in some cheesy song, though I do feel his presence when I listen to his 2014 album *The Traveler*. But I know that through his widow Wenndy MacKenzie (who incidentally is my vocal coach), and my memories of him, his spirit, like Roger's, will remain embedded in my soul.

---

18. Portions of my reflections about the loss of my long-time improv teacher were in my article "A Secular Grief Observed."

19

The Rise of the Nones

Cutting edge ventures used to draw in those disenchanted with traditional forms of church; however, as evidenced by the aforementioned statistics, attempts to rebrand church as "cool" and "cutting edge" no longer appeal to twenty-first century spiritual seekers. Conservative forms of religion, appealing to many, are appalling to many more, many of whom become "done" with religion and go on to live an entirely secular life. Some religion writers call secular people "nones," because that's what they put on the census forms under religion.

19. Hayward, "What to Wear Today."

People continue to exit from even the more progressively branded streams of Christianity that no longer speak to their values. Polls indicate that the majority of Americans do not support the "family values" agenda of the religious right.[20] But the will of the people remains silenced by both the political and religious institutions that define Americana Christianity. In their quest to preserve their place of pride, many Christian leaders appear to have forsaken the cardinal virtues that my ancestor possessed in spades.

With the exception of some small grassroots movements led largely by LGBTQ+ folks and people of color, even the more progressive forms of Christianity remain reluctant to embrace these positions.[21] They fear taking such "radical" stances will alienate their more conservative members and jeopardize their book sales

---

20. Historians such as Randall Balmer have well documented the religious right's "family values" agenda as focusing primarily on issues pertaining to human sexuality (especially their stances on "pro-life" and "homosexuality"). See Federman, "How US Evangelicals Fueled the Rise" for an analysis regarding how this belief system plays out in the current relationships been the United States and Russia. Meanwhile, the majority of Americans support abortion rights and marriage equality. See Pfeiffer, "Don't Be Fooled."

21. As one example of pseudo-progressivism in action, see Garrison, "Is SoJo a No-Go?" The almost universal silence from allegedly progressive Christian groups around issues relating to LGBTQ+ rights, reproductive rights, and human sexuality speaks volumes regarding their theology and funding streams. Also, interesting to note the proliferation of high end anti-poverty summits that are so pricey that only comfy Christians can afford to attend. Kind of hard to talk about ending poverty without actually engaging the poor, don't you think? See Sojourners' speaking fees as an example of this dynamic.

Having said this, one can exit this carnival as evidenced by Pavlovitz' book *A Bigger Table* and Barber and Lowery's book *Revive Us Again*. These books offer a positive vision for the future sans any apparent political and economic connections to the Christian Industrial Complex. (Though should said connections be proven down the road, I will revise this assessment.)

In addition, ventures led by atheists minister Gretta Vosper and ex-pastor Ryan Bell help guide secular spiritual seekers looking for community without the institutional faith trappings.

Also, a flurry of secular books such as Brown's *Pleasure Activism*, Hawken's *Blessed Unrest*, Klein's *No is Not Enough*, Reich's *The Common Good*, and Dionne's *One Nation After Trump* along with new media companies like Crooked Media offer positive suggestions for how to move collectively towards a more positive vision of the future.

and speaking gigs. Better to maintain one's platform by milking that Christian cow even if this object has now turned into a golden calf. It no longer matters what they believe, it matters what sells. More succinctly: money talks, and so they balk.

Of course, those peddling their politicized version of Christianity also hope you will buy not only their shtick, but their books, podcasts, and other spiritual swag as well. As a broke-ass religious satirist and storyteller, I have been tempted more than once to join them in peddling my wares to these missional masses. After all, such moves made millionaires out of the likes of megachurch pastors Rob Bell, Rick Warren, and Joel Osteen. Setting aside my inability to actually pen such faith fluff without losing my lunch, I am haunted by the astute words of the late comedian Bill Hicks. He aptly noted, "You do a commercial, you're off the artistic roll call forever. End of story, OK? You're another corporate shill, you're another whore at the capitalist gang bang."[22]

In his rant, Hicks acknowledges he will look the other way if a struggling artist takes the occasional commercialized gig because the rent money is overdue, they need to eat, and other basic necessities of life. Even my idol Carlin cut a commercial during a time of genuine financial hardship. But Hicks zeroes in on the proclivity for those in the spotlight to cash in on their talents by churning out what sells rather than what speaks to their heart. Over time, this spiritual spin cycle snuffs out the creative sparks that made their original work sing.[23] Carlin remains one of the few artists who could go commercial for a bit and then emerge with his integrity intact.

I confess that I also bought somewhat into my former peers' promotional strategies, as evidenced by a talk I gave at the UK Greenbelt Festival in 2007. "The New Atheist Crusaders and Their Unholy Grail" was based on a book by the same name released in 2008.[24] I wrote that book in large part because I thought if people

---

22. Hicks, "Artistic Roll Call."

23. I elaborate on the commercialization of Christian publishing in *Jesus Died for This?*, 37–42, portions of which were reprinted in "Jesus for Sale."

24. See Garrison, "The New Atheist Crusaders."

could only recognize the existence of a non-Gingrich God who doesn't proclaim Santorum-like spirituality, they would surely come over and see the light. If I could have known that this book project would end up edited with an eye toward Christianese, replete with a "evangelical"-branded PR campaign, I would have said no to this venture from the get-go.[25] Lessons learned.

Trying to "Christianize" a Carlin (or anyone else for that matter) proves to be not only an exercise in futility but also an act of outright cruelty. As written by my ancestor Roger, who attributed the words to a king: "Men's consciences ought in no sort to be violated, urged, or constrained."[26] Instead of this evangelical/emergent proclivity to convert the other over to their form of ungodly group-think, why can't we just embrace the mystery that is life? Whether one is a freethinking atheist, as Carlin was, or an apophatic agnostic Anglican like me, we need to be free to follow our souls as we understand them, unfettered from the sanctions of any governmental entity. For how can we have free will if organizations like The Family succeed in their quest to create a nation governed by their politicized version of right wing Christianity? This form of the faith privileges white male headship and promotes a worldview that sounds more *Handmaid's Tale* than heavenly.[27]

---

25. Even though *The Wittenburg Door* always lampooned the Christian subculture, there was a period when a few of us affiliated with the nation's oldest, largest and only religious satire magazine could find a way to work within the "Christian" market and still keep our integrity intact. But in the past few years, I have witnessed a significant shift by those publishers formerly known as edgy to appease their more conservative base (read: evangelicals/emergents desperate to prove they are both cool and Christian). This marketing decision to become "relevant" may fill their coffers temporarily as one can still find pockets of "holy hipsters" who will buy into this bible buzz. See Sargent, "Deconstructing the Christian Industrial Complex."

26. *The Bloudy Tenent*, 13.

27. See Gilbert, "Gilead in America" and Atwood, *The Handmaid's Tale*.

Return to Roger

Despite ongoing religious inspired rhetoric spewing from a range of self-professed political prayer warriors, could the tide be turning in Roger's direction? Methinks it might. For instance, with over half of Americans now in favor of marriage equality, this tells me those contemporary Puritans battling to preserve their version of "family values" already lost the war.[28] All signs indicate these Christian crusaders will continue to fight in the trenches as long as they receive media coverage and donations. As their battles linger on, expect them continuing to exhibit signs similar to the WWII era Japanese soldiers hiding in the hills who kept fighting an invisible war all by themselves long after Japan surrendered.[29]

As the 2016 Presidential election indicated, the war's not over yet. Far from it. Given the amount of money being funneled into evangelically minded political endeavors, I don't see any sign these prayer warriors will lay down their armor of God and give up the battle.[30] A daily scan of my RSS feeds tell me we're in the midst of a cultural hellfire that could burn us to the ground.

Yet, might we see a phoenix rising from the Americana ashes? Time will tell.

While the religious may call the "nones" and "dones" godless and soulless, I've observed for some time the emergence of secular communities that assume at least some of the familial, pastoral, and outreach roles traditionally performed by the institutional church. Also, online platforms such as meet-ups and private Facebook groups serve as hubs for those seeking community. In these groups they find a degree of privacy and security that allows conversations and connections to flourish without religious organizational involvement.[31]

---

28. See Pew Research Center, "Attitudes on Same-Sex Marriage."

29. See Taylan, "No Surrender-Japanese Holdouts."

30. For ongoing news regarding the latest in right wing funding, check out Right Wing Watch and the Southern Poverty Law Center. Also, see Ephesians 6:10–18 for the biblical verses discussing putting on the "armor of God."

31. To continue to learn more about the communities I find during my travels, connect with me via Twitter/Instagram @Becky_Garrison.

Now I would never advocate for the creation of a common ground where everyone comes together to sing Kumbaya and ponder our navels in search of some esoteric god-goo. Most of the time, these type of meetings tend to issue forth platitudes that might create a positive synergistic buzz for those present, but to the rest of the world, seem a Shakespearean mess: "Full of sound and fury, Signifying nothing."[32] On the rare occasion when they issue some kind of an actual resolution, their commentary tends to favor majority rule, thus casting aside those minority viewpoints who find themselves once again on the outside unable to have a voice at the inner table. Gatherings of this nature would probably send Roger running for the hills. I can hear the echoes of Carlin going off on one of his infamous hysterical rants against what he termed "self-righteous environmentalists; these white, bourgeois liberals."[33] Roger preferred the cacophony of disparate free thinkers arguing passionately in the public square to a group-think consensus.

Such arguments can indeed come to a limited consensus, not overwhelming all participants's individuality, but rather amplifying their voices on areas of common ground while acknowledging, respecting, even privileging their differences. As philosopher Martha Nussbaum observes, "The idea of an overlapping consensus, or, to put it Williams's way, the idea of a moral and natural goodness that we can share while differing on ultimate religious ends, is an idea that helps us think about our common life together much better than the unclear and at times misleading idea of separation."[34] To quote comedian, actor, marathon runner, and aspiring politician, Eddie Izzard, "I believe the melting pot is the thing that can save the world."[35] Although, maybe I'm talking less about author Israel Zangwill's 'melting pot' than about what former New York City mayor David Dinkins called a 'gorgeous mosaic.'[36]

32. *MacBeth*, Act V, Scene 5.
33. Carlin, "The Planet is Fine" (1992).
34. Nussbaum, *Liberty of Conscience*, 65.
35. Izzard, "Humanist Community at Harvard."
36. See Enyclopedia.com, "Melting Pot" and Roosevelt House, "A Mayor's

In an e-mail conversation, Brad Sargent (aka Futurist Guy) echoes a shift that I've been observing in recent years. "The nones and dones have moved towards creating sustainable and creative change starting at the grassroots level. They are seeking to reconnect the parts of humanity that have fragmented by joining together the analytic, mental, and physical parts of ourselves with our intuitive, emotional, and soul-spirit sides. They are creating reconnecting, placed-based meetings designed to search for transcendent meaning and real sustainable solutions."[37]

These communities seem to be embodying much of what missional (not only evangelical) Christianity has been doing: local, relational, community development, "neighboring." Sargent adds, "A number of my 'done' friends move into this kind of missional approach, without the institutionalized church as a base. A lot of them were previously paid staff or volunteer leaders in local churches where there was spiritual abuse–of them in particular, and of the everyday congregation members."[38]

While the nones and dones have been rising in numbers throughout the United States, I've noticing this trend most notably in the Pacific Northwest. Here one finds a steadfast spiritual connection to natural beauty. Separated from any professional connections to the Christian Industrial Complex and the growing branded atheist market, these spiritual seekers grow on their own sans any commercialized endeavors to brand and market their spiritual experiences.

Some of the communities I've encountered may sound like a church, but they're not. In fact, most of these folks will resist being identified with a "religious institution" though they're connecting to this spirit outside of ourselves that connects us to our global humanity.

Could these shifts be illuminating the larger theme of re-embodiment that puts back into the whole what US based Christianity split asunder from its inception? Within a decade at most,

---

Life."

37. Sargent, E-mail.
38. Sargent, E-mail.

could we live in a country where those who believe that LGBTQ+ folks do not deserve the same rights and rites as everyone else will be looked on as bigots? Along those lines, will grassroots movements like #blacklivesmatter and #metoo produce lasting change or just fade into the woodwork as yet another successful social media campaign?[39]

In my exploration of these progressive secular communities, I've become acutely aware of the elephant in the room that must be addressed. These communities may represent greater diversity in terms of gender identity and sexual orientation. Yet most of these gatherings still remain predominately white. Can those with privilege ever abandon the mic and truly listen to those who remain on the margins . . . who don't look like them?

Also, forming community is hard work, and time will tell which communities will endure in the long run. As these movements continue to grow, there is potential for abuse, similarly to the clergy scandals I've covered over the years. I've met my share of secular practitioners who misuse their positions of power to prey on the vulnerable. They can market themselves as mindful and yet remain clueless at best. Many display narcissistic and sociopathic tendencies.[40] Egos, cliques, and the like are all part of the human experience. So, discernment remains key moving forward.

> A friend of mine, Becky Garrison, who is a religion writer, has been talking about this reformation. She doesn't hold too much hope for the gradual approach. She says that there are alternative spiritual communities, "secular churches" so to speak, springing up. They aren't church, really. The participants wouldn't describe them as churches or as Christian. According to Becky, they fill the void left by those who left or who never

---

39. For a concise history of these movements, see Callahan, "Social Movements Likely to Dominate 2018." Also, see Vandermaas-Peeler, "Partisanship Trumps Gender" for an analysis regarding how issues like sexual harassment and access to contraception informed the 2018 midterm elections.

40. See Garrison, "Cutting the Cords of Toxic Relationships" for my reflections on the value of cord cutting as a tool to deal with those with narcissistic/sociopathic tendencies.

participated in the first place in traditional church communities. Becky puts it this way: "I need a community where people will care if I die." These are communities based on sacred dance/sexuality or improv, sustainable farming, even cannabis. More than a club or an interest group there is an ethic about them, a need to give something to the world, to touch heart, discover authenticity, to accept those left out, to care when one in their community dies. To touch.

—JOHN SHUCK, host, Progressive Spirit podcast[41]

Like Roger before me, I've become a seeker who is no longer saved but still searches. The more I connect with spiritual atheists, agnostics, and religious exiles banished from the institutional church both living and dead, the more I realize that while we all think for ourselves, we often speak a similar language at our core that connects us together in our shared humanity. In connecting with our common humanity through these spiritual movements, we ignite a spark. That spark can create embers to fuel a fire.

If those with privilege can truly learn to hear the other, perhaps we can bring forth the creation of truly inclusive communities that can welcome all. Then we can explore how to live together in a virtuous and not a vicious society, where all can be free to exercise their liberty of conscience, while caring for all. That was the world Roger strove virtuously to achieve. Though he did not succeed in the eyes of his contemporaries, he left behind a legacy of a fiery, kind, and compassionate warrior willing to fight to the end to grant us all the right to worship as we please.

To this end, I hope for the day when we can all say "Amen."

---

41. Shuck, "Jesus As Ishta Deva."

42

Every day people are straying away from the church and going back to God.
— Lenny Bruce[43]

42. Hayward, "Creationism Meets Evolution."
43. Bruce, "Christ and Moses," 215.

Bibliography

19 Kids and Counting. Silver Spring, MD: The Learning Channel, 2008–15.
Arnold, Samuel Greene. *History of the State of Rhode Island and Providence Plantations*, vol. 1. New York: D. Appleton & Co., 1859.
Art of Being. https://artofbeing.com.
Atwood, Margaret. *The Handmaid's Tale*. 2nd ed. New York: Houghton Mifflin Harcourt, 2017.
Bad Religion. "American Jesus." Track 3 on *A Recipe for Hate*. New York: Atlantic Records Group, 1993, CD.
Backus, Isaac. *A History of New England with particular reference to the denomination of Christians called Baptists*. Boston, MA: Edward Draper, 1777.
Balmer, Randall. *Thy Kingdom Come*. New York: Basic, 2006.
———. "Under Trump, America's Religious Right is Rewriting its Code of Ethics." *The Guardian* (February 18, 2018). http://www.theguardian.com/commentisfree/2018/feb/18/donald-trump-evangelicals-code-of-ethics.
Bailyn, Bernard. *The Barbarous Years: The Peopling of British North America—The Conflict of Civilizations, 1600-1675*. New York: Knopf, 2013.
Barber II, William J. and Lowery, Rick. *Revive Us Again: Vision and Action in Moral Organizing*. Boston: Beacon Press, 2018.
Barnett, Wayne. *The Greatest Show on Earth*. New York: Regan, 2016.
Barry, John M. "God, Government and Roger Williams' Big Idea." *Smithsonian Magazine* (January 2012). http://www.smithsonianmag.com/history/god-government-and-roger-williams-big-idea-6291280.
———. *Roger Williams and the Creation of the American Soul: Church, State, and the Birth of Liberty*. New York: Viking, 2012.
———. "Roger Williams, America's First Rebel." *The Nation*. (May 2, 2012). http://www.thenation.com/article/roger-williams-americas-first-rebel.
Baysinger, Tim. "Flashback: Bill Cosby and Roseanne Had TV's Top-Rated Shows for 2 Straight Years in Late '80s." *The Wrap* (May 30, 2018). http://www.thewrap.com/flashback-bill-cosby-and-roseanne-had-tvs-two-top-rated-shows-for-2-straight-years-in-late-80s.

BIBLIOGRAPHY

Bell, J.L. "No Taxation Without Representation." *Journal of the American Revolution* (May 23, 2013). http://allthingsliberty.com/2013/05/no-taxation-without-representation-part-2.

Bell, Ryan. https://www.patreon.com/lifeaftergod.

Blumberg, Jess. "A Brief History of the Salem Witch Trials," *Smithsonian* (October 23, 2007). http://www.smithsonianmag.com/history-archaeology/brief-salem.html.

Bronner, Ethan. "Religious Groups and Employers Battle Contraception Mandate." *New York Times* (January 23, 2013). http://www.nytimes.com/2013/01/27/health/religious-groups-and-employers-battle-contraception-mandate.html.

Brown, Adrienne Maree. *Pleasure Activism: The Politics of Feeling Good.* Chico, CA: AK Press, 2019.

Brown, DeNeen. "The Preacher Who Used Christianity to Revive the Ku Klux Klan." *The Washington Post* (April 10, 2018). http://www.washingtonpost.com/news/retropolis/wp/2018/04/08/the-preacher-who-used-christianity-to-revive-the-ku-klux-klan.

Boston, Rob. E-mail, July 2012. http://www.au.org.

Bruce, Lenny. "Christ and Moses." In *The Big Book of Jewish Humor,* edited by William Novak and Moshe Waldocks, 215. New York: Harper Collins, 1980.

Bruckner, Edward M. and Bruckner, Michael E. *In Freedom We Trust.* Amherst, MA: Prometheus, 2012.

Burgo, Joseph. *The Narcissist You Know.* New York: Touchstone, 2015.

Burleigh, Nina. "Tump and White Evangelicals: Support for President Grows, but Millennials Leave Movement." *Newsweek* (April 14, 2018). http://www.newsweek.com/trump-evangelicals-support-millennials-888267.

Callahan, Molly, "#Metoo, #Blacklivesmatter, #Nobannowall: Social Movements Likely to Dominate 2018." *News@Northwestern* (January 7, 2018). http://news.northeastern.edu/2018/01/12/metoo-blacklivesmatter-nobannowall-social-movements-likely-to-dominate-2018.

Carlin, George. "Religion." *You Are all Diseased.* New York: NY: HBO, 1999.

———. "Why We Don't Need 10 Commandments." *Complaints and Grievances.* New York: NY: HBO, 2001.

Carlin, Kelly. "A Carlin Home Companion." http://thekellycarlinsite.com/speaking/solo-show.

Carpenter, Edmund James. *Roger Williams: A Study of the Life, Times and Character of a Political Pioneer.* New York: The Grafton, 1909.

Carter Roger Williams Initiative. "A Key into the Language of America." http://www.findingrogerwilliams.com/essays/an-essay-on-a-key-into-the-language-of-america.

———. "Original Land Deed to Providence." http://www.findingrogerwilliams.com/maps/original_deed.html.

Catholic Answers. "Tract: Birth Control" (November 11, 2018). http://www.catholic.com/tract/birth-control.

BIBLIOGRAPHY

Cheng, Patrick. *Rainbow Theology: Bridging Race, Sexuality, and Spirit*. New York: Seabury, 2013.
Christianity.com. "Mary Dyer Hanged for 'Wrong' Faith." http://www.christianity.com/church/church-history/timeline/1601-1700/mary-dyer-hanged-for-wrong-faith-11630131.html.
The Clergy Project. http://clergyproject.org.
Comte-Sponville, André. *The Little Book of Atheist Spirituality*. New York: Viking, 2007.
———. *A Small Treatise on the Great Virtues: The Uses of Philosophy in Everyday Life*. New York: Metropolitan, 2001.
Constitution Society. "The Examination of Mrs. Anne Hutchinson at the Court at Newton, 1637." http://www.constitution.org/primarysources/hutchinson.html.
Cotton, John. *The Bloudy Tenent, Washed and Made White in the Bloud of the Lambe (1647)*. Whitefish, MT: Kessinger, 2003.
Cox, Daniel and Jones, Robert P. "America's Changing Religious Identity." *PRRI* (September 6, 2017). http://www.prri.org/research/american-religious-landscape-christian-religiously-unaffiliated.
Crane, Stephen. *The Red Badge of Courage*. New York: D. Appleton & Co., 1895.
Crooked Media. https://crooked.com.
"The Darwin Awards." https://darwinawards.com.
Davis, Kenneth. "America's True History of Religious Tolerance." *Smithsonian Magazine* (October 2010). https://www.smithsonianmag.com/history/americas-true-history-of-religious-tolerance-61312684.
de Botton, Alain. *Religion for Atheists*. New York: Pantheon, 2012.
Dexter, Henry Martyn. *As to Roger Williams and his Banishment of the Massachusetts Plantation*. Boston: Congregational Publishing Society, 1876.
Dione, E. J. *One Nation After Trump*. New York: St. Martin's Press, 2017.
Drogin, Bob. "'Rogues' Island' Lives Up to Nickname : Big Scandals Help Mark Tiniest State's 350th Year," *LA Times* (May 15, 1986). https://www.latimes.com/archives/la-xpm-1986-05-15-mn-5160-story.html.
Dylan, Bob. "The Times They Are a-Changin'." Track 1 on *The Times They Are a-Changin'*. Columbia, 1964, vinyl.
Elton, Romeo. *Life of Roger Williams: The Earliest Legislator and True Champion for a Full Liberty of Conscience*. Providence: G.H. Whitney, 1853.
Encyclopedia Britannica. "William Coddington." https://www.britannica.com/biography/William-Coddington.
———. "William Laud." https://www.britannica.com/biography/William-Laud.
Encyclopedia.com. "Melting Pot." http://www.encyclopedia.com/history/united-states-and-canada/us-history/melting-pot.
Escobar, Kathy. *Down We Go: Living Into the Wild Ways of Jesus*. San Jose, CA: Civitas, 2011.
Estep, William R. *Revolution Within the Revolution*. Grand Rapids: William B. Eerdmans, 1990.

Fadel, Angie. http://angiefadel.com.
Farmers' Almanac. https://www.farmersalmanac.com.
Fea, John. "Evangelical Fear Elected Trump." *The Atlantic* (June 24, 2018). http://www.theatlantic.com/ideas/archive/2018/06/a-history-of-evangelical-fear/563558.
Federman, Adam "How US Evangelicals Fueled the Rise of Russia's 'Pro-Family' Right." *The Nation* (January 7, 2014). http://www.thenation.com/article/how-us-evangelicals-fueled-rise-russias-pro-family-right.
"The First Muslims in England." *The BBC Magazine* (March 20, 2016). https://www.bbc.com/news/magazine-35843991.
Fitzgerald, Frances. *The Evangelicals*. New York: Simon and Schuster, 2017.
Follman, Mark, et al. "US Mass Shootings, 1982-2019: Data From Mother Jones' Investigation" *Mother Jones* (May 31, 2019). https://www.motherjones.com/politics/2012/12/mass-shootings-mother-jones-full-data.
Flynn, Eileen, "Q&A: Author Becky Garrison talks mission-shaped ministries and unbiblical BS." *The Grand Scheme* (November 17, 2011). http://eileenflynn.wordpress.com/2011/11/17/qa-author-becky-garrison-talks-mission-shaped-ministries-and-unbiblical-bs.
Friends General Conference. "FAQs about Quakers." https://www.fgcquaker.org/discover/faqs-about-quakers.
Gammel, William. *Life of Roger Williams*. Boston: Gould and Lincoln, 1854.
Garrison, Becky. "#churchtoo." *The Baffler* (May 21, 2018). https://thebaffler.com/latest/churchtoo-garrison.
———. *Ancient Future Disciples: Meeting Jesus in Mission-Shaped Ministries*. New York, NY: Seabury, 2011.
———. "Atheist Pastor Deemed Unsuitable for Ministry." *TheHumanist.com* (October 4, 2016). http://thehumanist.com/news/religion/atheist-pastor-deemed-unsuitable-ministry.
———. "Christ and Capitalism: Cashing In on the Merger of Church and State." *Paste Magazine* (June 14, 2017). http://www.pastemagazine.com/articles/2017/06/christ-and-capitalism-cashing-in-on-the-merger-of.html.
———. "Coming Home to a Carlin Companion: Connecting with the Spirit of George." *American Atheist*, 2nd & 3rd Quarter, 2012.
———. "Cutting the Cords of Toxic Relationships." *Grok Nation* (February 6, 2017). http://groknation.com/soul/cutting-cord.
———."Deconstructing Dominionism." *American Atheist*, 4th Quarter, 2011.
———. "Embracing the Six Types Of Love." *Role Reboot* (July 14, 2017). http://www.rolereboot.org/sex-and-relationships/details/2017-07-embracing-six-types-love.
———. "Experiments in Accountability, Forgiveness, and Reconciliation." *God's Politics blog* (January 11, 2010). http://sojo.net/blogs/2010/01/11/experiments-accountability-forgiveness-and-reconciliation.
———. "The Family: More Gilead than Godly." *TheHumanist.com* (August 6, 2019). https://thehumanist.com/arts_entertainment/culture/the-family-more-gilead-than-godly.

———. "From Ronald to the Donald: What in God's Name Happened?" *Medium* (October 24, 2018). http://medium.com/@becky_garrison/from-ronald-to-the-donald-what-in-gods-name-happened-6aa2478bfec2.
———. "Is SoJo a No-Go on LGBTQ Equality?" *God's Politics Blog* (May 11, 2011). http://killingthebuddha.com/ktblog/is-sojo-a-no-go-on-lgbtq-equality.
———. *Jesus Died for This?* Grand Rapids, MI: Zondervan, 2010.
———. "Jesus for Sale." *Killing the Buddha* (August 10, 2010). http://killingthebuddha.com/mag/dispatch/jesus-for-sale.
———. "Lots of Love: Exploring Polyamory in Portland." *The Humanist* (February 19, 2019). https://thehumanist.com/magazine/march-april-2019/features/lots-of-love-exploring-polyamory-in-portland.
———. "The New Atheist Crusaders and their Unholy Grail." *Greenbelt UK* (2007). http://www.greenbelt.org.uk/talks/the-new-atheist-crusaders-their-unholy-grail.
———. *The New Atheist Crusaders and their Unholy Grail*. Nashville: Thomas Nelson, 2008.
———. "An Obituary for Right-Wing Evangelicalism." *Religion Dispatches* (December 26, 2012). http://religiondispatches.org/an-obituary-for-right-wing-evangelicalism.
———. "The Pope vs. Spiderman." *WittenburgDoor.com* (April 21, 2008). http://www.wittenburgdoor.com/pope-vs-spiderman.html.
———. *Red and Blue God, Black and Blue Church*. San Francisco: Jossey Bass, 2006.
———. "Rise of the Party of Nones." *TheHumanist.com* (May 26, 2016). http://thehumanist.com/commentary/rise-party-nones.
———. "A Secular Grief Observed." *American Atheist*, 2nd Quarter, 2018, revised version posted on *Killing the Buddha* (June 7, 2011). http://killingthebuddha.com/ktblog/a-secular-grief-observed.
———. "'Soul Freedom' Versus 'Christian Nation:' Exploring the Legacy of Roger Williams." *Religion Dispatches* (September 20, 2010). http://religiondispatches.org/soul-freedom-versus-christian-nation-exploring-the-legacy-of-roger-williams.
———. "Surveying the Demise of White American Christianity." *TheHumanist.com* (September 14, 2017). http://thehumanist.com/news/religion/surveying-demise-white-american-christianity.
Gaustad, Edwin. *Roger Williams*. New York: Oxford University Press, 2001.
Gilbert, Sophie. "Gilead in America." *The Atlantic* (June 20, 2018). http://www.theatlantic.com/entertainment/archive/2018/06/gilead-in-america/563141.
Goddard, Ian. "Roger Williams: Champion of Liberty." *Goddard's Journal*. http://www.iangoddard.com/roger.htm.
Godwin, Mike. "Meme, Counter-meme," *Wired* (October 1994). https://www.wired.com/1994/10/godwin-if-2.
Hare, Robert D. *Without Conscience*. New York: Guilford, 1999.

Hawken, Paul. *Blessed Unrest: How the Largest Social Movement in History Is Restoring Grace, Justice, and Beauty to the World*. New York: Penguin Books, 2007.

Hayward, David. "Are Trump and the Church in Bed Together?" *NakedPastor* (August 14, 2017). https://nakedpastor.com/are-trump-and-the-church-in-bed-together.

———. "Cartoon: Tell the Difference." *NakedPastor* (March 31, 2011). https://www.patheos.com/blogs/nakedpastor/2011/03/cartoon-tell-the-difference.

———. "Deciding What to Wear." *NakedPastor* (March 20, 2017). https://www.nakedpastor.com/vacation-mode-and-what-to-wear.

———. "International Women's Day 2018: Are Smart Women Evil?" *NakedPastor* (March 8, 2018). https://nakedpastor.com/international-womens-day-2018-are-smart-women-evil.

———. "Not Going in There with All Those Homosexuals!" *NakedPastor* (June 5, 2018). https://nakedpastor.com/not-going-in-there-with-all-those-homosexuals

———. "Tee Shirt Idea: Creation Meets Evolution." *NakedPastor* (April 14, 2008). https://nakedpastor.com/tee-shirt-idea-creationism-meets-evolution.

Hicks, Bill. "Artistic Roll Call." Track 19 on *Rant in E-Minor*. Salem, MA: Rykodisc, 1997, CD.

I AM: Trans People Speak. http://www.transpeoplespeak.org.

Inazu, John. "Do Black Lives Matter to Evangelicals?" *The Washington Post* (January 6, 2016). http://www.washingtonpost.com/news/acts-of-faith/wp/2016/01/05/do-black-lives-matter-to-evangelicals.

It Gets Better. https://itgetsbetter.org.

Izzard, Eddie. "Eddie Izzard Accepts the Outstanding Lifetime Achievement Award in Cultural Humanism." *Humanist Community at Harvard* (February 20, 2013, video uploaded February 23, 2013). https://vimeo.com/60515051.

Jacoby, Susan. "The White House is Tearing Down the Wall Between Church and State." *New York Times* (July 5, 2018). http://www.nytimes.com/2018/07/05/opinion/sunday/church-state-supreme-court-religion.html.

James, Aaron. *The Narcissist Next Door*. New York: Riverhead, 2014.

James, Sydney. *John Clarke and His Legacies: Religion and Law in Colonial Rhode Island, 1638–1750*. University Park, PA: Pennsylvania State University Press, 1999.

Johnston, David Cay. *The Making of Donald Trump*. Brooklyn: Melville House, 2016.

Joyce, Rosemary. "Coupling and Culture." *Psychology Today* (February 4, 2012). https://www.psychologytoday.com/us/blog/what-makes-us-human/201202/coupling-and-culture.

Kendi, Ibram X. *How to Be an Antiracist*. New York: One World, 2019.

———. *Stamped from the Beginning: The Definitive History of Racist Ideas in America*. New York: Bold Type, 2017.

King, Henry Melville. *Sir Henry Vane, Jr.: Governor of Massachusetts and Friend of Roger Williams and Rhode Island.* Providence: Preston & Rounds Co., 1909.

Klein, Naomi. *No is Not Enough.* Chicago: Haymarket, 2017.

Knowles, James D. *Memoir of Roger Williams,* Boston: Lincoln, Edmonds & Co.,1834.

Kranish, Michael and Fisher, Marc. *Trump Revealed: The Definitive Biography of the 45th President.* New York: Scribner, 2016.

Lee, Bandy. *The Dangerous Case of Donald Trump: 27 Psychiatrists and Mental Health Experts Assess a President.* New York, NY: Thomas Dunne, 2017.

Lehman, Chris. *The Money Cult: Capitalism, Christianity and the Unmasking of the American Dream.* Brooklyn: Melville House, 2017.

Lehrer, Tom. "The Vatican Rag." Track 14 on *That Was the Year That Was.* Shout!, 1965, vinyl.

Let Fury Have the Hour. Directed by Antonino D'Ambrosio. New York: Tribeca Film Festival, 2012. http://www.tribecafilm.com/filmguide/archive/512cfoda1c7d76e0460015e9-let-fury-have-the-hour.

Levin, Ira. *The Stepford Wives.* New York: Random House, 1972.

The Lion King, Directed by Roger Allers and Rob Minkoff. Burbank, CA: Walt Disney Co., 1994.

Lipka, Michael. "Many U.S. Congregations are Still Racially Segregated, But Things are Changing." *Pew Research Center* (December 8, 2014). https://www.pewresearch.org/fact-tank/2014/12/08/many-u-s-congregations-are-still-racially-segregated-but-things-are-changing-2.

Longfellow, Henry Wadsworth. *The Courtship of Miles Standish.* Indianapolis: Bobbs-Merrill Company, 1858.

MacKenzie, Jason. *Psychopath Free.* New York: Berkeley, 2015.

Mak, Tim. "Occupy Wall St. Copies Arab Spring." *Politico* (October 3, 2011). http://www.politico.com/news/stories/1011/64993.html.

Malkin, Craig. *Rethinking Narcissism.* New York: Harper Perennial, 2015.

Martinez, Jessica and Smith Gregory. "How the Faithful Voted: A Preliminary 2016 Analysis." *Pew Research Center* (November 6, 2016). http://www.pewresearch.org/fact-tank/2016/11/09/how-the-faithful-voted-a-preliminary-2016-analysis.

Marxists Internet Archive. "The Peasants' Revolt, 1381." http://www.marxists.org/history/england/peasants-revolt/story.htm.

Mashantucket Pequot Museum & Resource Center. "Battlefields of the Pequot War." http://pequotwar.org.

McLain, Lisa. "How the Catholic Church Came to Oppose Birth Control." *The Conversation.* http://theconversation.com/how-the-catholic-church-came-to-oppose-birth-control-95694.

The Miller Center. "McCarthyism and the Red Scare." https://millercenter.org/the-presidency/educational-resources/age-of-eisenhower/mcarthyism-red-scare.

Miller, Perry. "An Essay In Interpretation." In *The Complete Writings of Roger Williams*, vol. VII. Eugene, OR: Wipf & Stock, 2007.

Milligan, Susan. "Once Skeptical, the Religious Right is Now Singing the Praises of President Donald Trump." *US News & World Report* (May 5, 2017). http://www.usnews.com/news/the-report/articles/2017-05-05/president-trumps-spiritual-journey-delivers-for-the-religious-right.

Monty Python. "Bruces' Philosophers Song (The Bruces Song.)" Track 16 on *Monty Python Sings*. Virgin Records, 1989, vinyl.

Monty Python's Flying Circus. London: BBC, 1969-74.

Morris, Maxwell H. "Roger Williams and the Jews" (1951). http://americanjewisharchives.org/publications/journal/PDF/1951_03_02_00_morris.pdf.

The National Archives. "13th Amendment to the U.S. Constitution: Abolition of Slavery." https://www.archives.gov/historical-docs/13th-amendment.

———. "19th Amendment to the U.S. Constitution: Women's Right to Vote." https://www.archives.gov/historical-docs/19th-amendment.

Native American Journalists Association (NAJA), "Reporting and Indigenous Terminology." https://najanewsroom.com/wp-content/uploads/2018/11/NAJA_Reporting_and_Indigenous_Terminology_Guide.pdf.

National Parks Service: Roger Williams National Memorial. "Frequently Asked Questions." http://www.nps.gov/rowi/faqs.htm.

———. "Liberty of Conscience." http://www.nps.gov/rowi/index.htm.

———. "Roger Williams: King Philip's War." http://www.nps.gov/rowi/historyculture/philipswar.htm.

———. "Roger Williams: Youth & Education." http://www.nps.gov/rowi/historyculture/youth.htm.

———. "The Tree Root That Ate Roger Williams." http://www.nps.gov/rowi/learn/news/the-tree-root-that-ate-roger-williams.htm.

Neilson. Kurt. E-mail, September 2012.

Nelson, Anne. *Shadow Network: Media, Money, and the Secret Hub of the Radical Right*. New York: Bloomsbury Publishing, 2019.

New England Historical Society. "Obadiah Holmes, The Baptist Martyr The Puritans Should Have Left Alone." http://www.newenglandhistoricalsociety.com/obadiah-holmes-baptist-martyr-puritans.

The New World Encyclopedia. "Anne Hutchinson." http://www.newworldencyclopedia.org/entry/Anne_Hutchinson.

Newell, Jim. "Trump Answers Prayers." *Slate* (May 3, 2018). https://slate.com/news-and-politics/2018/05/trump-is-giving-the-religious-right-exactly-what-it-wants.html.

Nodal, Kate, "Slavery Affects More than 40 Million People Worldwide–More Than at Any Other Time in History." *The Guardian* (February 25, 2017). https://www.theguardian.com/news/2019/feb/25/modern-slavery-trafficking-persons-one-in-200.

Nussbaum, Martha. *Liberty of Conscience*. New York: Basic, 2010.

Panetta, Grade and Reaney, Olivia. "The Evolution of American Voting Rights in 242 Years Shows How Far We've Come—And How Far We Still Have To Go." *Business Insider* (February 15, 2019). https://www.businessinsider.com/when-women-got-the-right-to-vote-american-voting-rights-timeline-2018-10.

Past Tense. "Bartholomew Legate Burnt for Heresy (1612)." http://pasttenseblog.wordpress.com/2016/03/18/today-in-londons-religious-history-bartholomew-legate-burnt-for-heresy-1612.

Pavlovitz, John. *A Bigger Table*. Louisville, KY: Westminster John Knox Press (2017).

Public Broadcasting Service. "God in America: People and Ideas: Early American Individuals." October 2010. http://www.pbs.org/wgbh/americanexperience/features/godinamerica-early-american-individuals.

Pew Research Center. "Attitudes on Same-Sex Marriage." (May 14, 2019). http://www.pewforum.org/fact-sheet/changing-attitudes-on-gay-marriage.

Pfeiffer, Eric. "Don't Be Fooled: Most Americans Agree on Abortion, Guns, and Other Heated Issues." *Upworthy* (July 3, 2018). http://www.upworthy.com/don-t-be-fooled-most-americans-agree-on-abortion-guns-and-other-heated-issues.

Portland Abbey Arts. http://www.facebook.com/portlandabbeyarts.

Prothero, Stephen. *American Jesus*. New York, NY: Farrar, Straus and Giroux, 2003.

Puls, Darrell and Gall, Glenn. "Frequency of Narcissistic Personality Disorder in Pastors." *Research Gate* (September 2015). http://www.researchgate.net/publication/282354802_Frequency_of_Narcissistic_Personality_Disorder_in_Pastors.

Renaud, Myriam. "Myths Debunked: Why Did White Evangelicals Vote for Trump?" *Martin Marty Center for the Public Understanding of Religion: University of Chicago Divinity School* (January 19, 2017). http://divinity.uchicago.edu/sightings/myths-debunked-why-did-white-evangelical-christians-vote-trump.

Rhode Island Department of State. "Charter of Rhode Island" (1663). http://sos.ri.gov/divisions/Civics-And-Education/teacher-resources/rhode-island-charter.

Right Wing Watch. http://www.rightwingwatch.org.

Rodgers, Daniel T. *As a City on a Hill: The Story of America's Most Famous Lay Sermon*. Princeton: Princeton University Press, 2018.

Rogers, Kenny. "The Gambler," Track 13 on *The Kenny Rogers Single Album*, United Artists, 1979, vinyl.

Roosevelt House Public Policy Institute at Hunter College, City University of New York. "A Mayor's Life: Governing New York's Gorgeous Mosaic." (October 21, 2013). http://www.roosevelthouse.hunter.cuny.edu/events/david-dinkins-mayors-life-governing-new-yorks-gorgeous-mosaic.

Roth, Gabrielle. *5Rhythms*. https://www.5rhythms.com/gabrielle-roths-5rhythms.

Rowan & Martin's Laugh In. Created by George Schlatter. Los Angeles: NBC, 1967-73.

Sargent, Brad. "Deconstructing the Christian Industrial Complex." *futuristguy.* https://futuristguy.wordpress.com/deconstructing-the-christian-industrial-complex-compilation-of-posts.

———. E-mail, February 2017.

Schwadel, Philip and Smith, Gregory A. "Evangelical approval of Trump remains high, but other religious groups are less supportive." *Pew Research Center* (March 18, 2019). https://www.pewresearch.org/fact-tank/2019/03/18/evangelical-approval-of-trump-remains-high-but-other-religious-groups-are-less-supportive.

Sedaka, Neil. "Happy Birthday Sweet Sixteen" (1961).

Shakespeare, William. *MacBeth*. New York: Samuel French, 1918.

Shuck, John. "Jesus As Ishta Deva." *Southminster Presbyterian Church* (October 9, 2016). https://www.southmin.org/multimedia-archive/jesus-as-ishta-deva.

———. "Progressive Spirit: Becky Garrison, Secular Church." *KBOO* (October 10, 2016). https://kboo.fm/media/53066-becky-garrison-secular-church.

Singer, Mark. *Trump and Me*. New York: Tim Dugan, 2016.

"Sojourners Speakers Bureau: Information and Guidelines." https://sojo.net/speakers-bureau-information-and-guidelines.

Southern Baptist Conference. "On 'Same-Sex Marriage' And Civil Rights Rhetoric." (2012). http://www.sbc.net/resolutions/1224/on-samesex-marriage-and-civil-rights-rhetoric.

Southern Poverty Law Center. "White Lives Matter." https://www.splcenter.org/fighting-hate/extremist-files/group/white-lives-matter.

Star Wars. Directed by George Lucas. Los Angeles: The Walt Disney Company (via Lucasfilms), 1977.

State Library of Massachusetts. "Mayflower Passengers." https://archives.lib.state.ma.us/bitstream/handle/2452/208249/ocn137336369-Mayflower-passengers.pdf?sequence=3&isAllowed=y.

Stepford Wives Organization. http://www.stepfordwife.com.

Strickland, Arthur Barsazou. *Roger Williams: Prophet and Pioneer of Soul-Liberty*. New York: Judson, 1919.

Straus, Oscar S. *Roger Williams: The Pioneer of Religious Liberty*. New York: The Century Company, 1894.

Stout, Martha. *The Sociopath Next Door*. New York: Harmony, 2006.

SXSW. "Bridging the Digital and the Divine." (2012). http://schedule.sxsw.com/2012/events/event_IAP8710.

Taylan, Justin. "No Surrender-Japanese Holdouts." http://www.wanpela.com/holdouts/index.html.

True Woman.™ http://www.reviveourhearts.com/true-woman.

USA Postage Stamps. "3c Rhode Island Tercentenary statue of Roger Williams 1936." http://www.usapostagestamps.com/top_rated/overall/452/3c+Rhode+Island+Tercentenary+statue+of+Roger+Williams+1936.

BIBLIOGRAPHY

Vandermaas-Peeler, Alex, et al. "Partisanship Trumps Gender: Sexual Harassment, Woman Candidates, Access to Contraception, and Key Issues in 2018 Midterms." *PRRI* (October 2, 2018). https://www.prri.org/research/abortion-reproductive-health-midterms-trump-kavanaugh.
Vosper, Gretta. https://www.grettavosper.ca.
Vowell, Sarah. *The Wordy Shipmates*. New York: Riverhead, 2008.
Waldman, Steve. *Founding Faith*. New York: Random House, 2009.
———. *Sacred Liberty*. San Francisco, CA: Harper One, 2019.
Wall Street. Directed by Oliver Stone. Los Angeles: 20th Century Fox, 1987.
Walt, Stephen M. "The Myth of American Exceptionalism." *Foreign Policy* (October 11, 2011). http://foreignpolicy.com/2011/10/11/the-myth-of-american-exceptionalism.
Ward, Karen. E-mail, August 2019.
Williams, Roger. *The Bloudy Tenent of Persecution for Cause of Conscience*, edited by Edward Bean Underhill for the Harry Knowles Society. London: Haddon, 1848.
———. *The Bloody Tenent Yet More Bloody: by Mr Cottons endevour to wash it white in the Blood of the Lambe*. London: Giles Calvert, 1652.
———. *Experiments of Spiritual Health and Life and Preservatives* (1652). London: Sidney & Rider, 1863.
———. *George Fox Digged Out of His Burrowes* (1676). Whitefish, MT: Kessinger, 2003.
———. *A Key to the Language of America, or a help to the Languages of the Natives in that part of America Called New-England that part of America Called New-England*. London: Gregory Dexter, 1643.
———. "Letter to the Town of Providence Roger Williams, 1655." https://corematerials.homestead.com/13_Letter_to_the_Town_of_Providence.pdf.
Winship, Michael P. *Godly Republicanism*. Cambridge, MA: Harvard University Press, 2012.
Winthrop, John. "City upon a Hill," 1630. http://www.gilderlehrman.org/sites/default/files/inline-pdfs/Winthrop%27s%20City%20upon%20a%20Hill.pdf
Wokeck, Marianne S. and Coleman Martin A., eds. *The Works of George Santayana*, vol. 7, bk. I. Cambridge, MA: MIT Press, 2013.
Wolpe, David "Here's Who Donald Trump Would Be in the Bible." *Time* (March 15, 2016). http://time.com/4258270/donald-trump-king-david.
Zeitz, Joshua. "How Trump Is Making Us Rethink American Exceptionalism." *Politico* (January 7, 2018). http://www.politico.com/magazine/story/2018/01/07/trump-american-exceptionalism-history-216253.
Zoglin, Richard. "How George Carlin Changed Comedy." *Time* (June 23, 2008). http://content.time.com/time/arts/article/0,8599,1817192,00.html.
Zuckerman, Phil, "The Trump Administration's Alternative Christianity." *LA Times* (August 11, 2017). http://www.latimes.com/opinion/op-ed/la-oe-zuckerman-christians-trump-administration-20170811-story.html.

www.ingramcontent.com/pod-product-compliance
Lightning Source LLC
Chambersburg PA
CBHW070302100426
42743CB00011B/2317